bill bowler
sue parminter

move

elementary

coursebook
with CD-ROM

move elementary contents map

Module 1 Worldwide

Module 2 Ourselves

Module 3 Choices

Unit	Topic	Language study	Vocabulary	Main skills
1 **See the world** pages 66–69	• Around the world • On the move (travel and transport)	• Talking about life experiences (the present perfect simple)	• Holiday activities • Words related to travel and transport	• **Reading:** transferring key information • **Pronunciation:** connected speech • **Speaking:** making travel arrangements • **Listening:** identifying the situation in dialogues
2 **Market place** pages 70–73	• Buy me! (the power of advertising) • All in a name (well-known companies and their names)	• Comparing things: comparative and superlative adjectives	• Adjectives to describe a product • Business words	• **Listening:** understanding key information • **Reading:** checking predictions • **Speaking:** comparing a variety of products; giving a short presentation
3 **Outdoor life** pages 74–77	• Working with the weather (an interview with a weatherman) • What's the weather like?	• Present tenses and future plans (present simple and present continuous for future plans)	• The weather	• **Reading:** understanding main information • **Speaking:** conducting a simple interview; planning a visit to an event • **Listening:** identifying weather conditions
4 **Advances** pages 78–81	• Inventions (favourite and least favourite inventions) • Into the future (a chat forum)	• Talking about the future (expressing future intentions with *going to*)	• Modern inventions • Phrasal verbs: discovery and development	• **Listening:** identifying main ideas in a radio programme • **Pronunciation:** diphthongs • **Speaking:** giving and justifying opinions; talking about future plans • **Reading:** understanding and responding to main ideas • **Writing:** an interactive class chat forum

5 **Review unit** pages 82–85
- **Extra practice** pages 86–89 • **Grammar reference and wordlist** pages 90–92 • **Listening scripts:** pages 94–95 • **Communication activities:** pages 93, 96
- **Use CD2 for listening activities in the module**

CD-ROM

Location	• Modules 1–3, Units 1–4
Activities for each unit	• Language activity • Vocabulary activity • Common European Framework linked activity • Language game
Features	• Markbook – helps you to record and update your marks. • Bookmark – helps you to save your favourite activities. • Wordlist – helps you to create your own wordlists. • You can back up, restore and print out your Markbook, Bookmarks and Wordlists. You can also send saved files as emails. • For more information use the Help feature.

move elementary at a glance

In the Coursebook:

three 32-page modules

On the CD-ROM:

48 language activities and games, a help section and markbook, wordlist and bookmark features

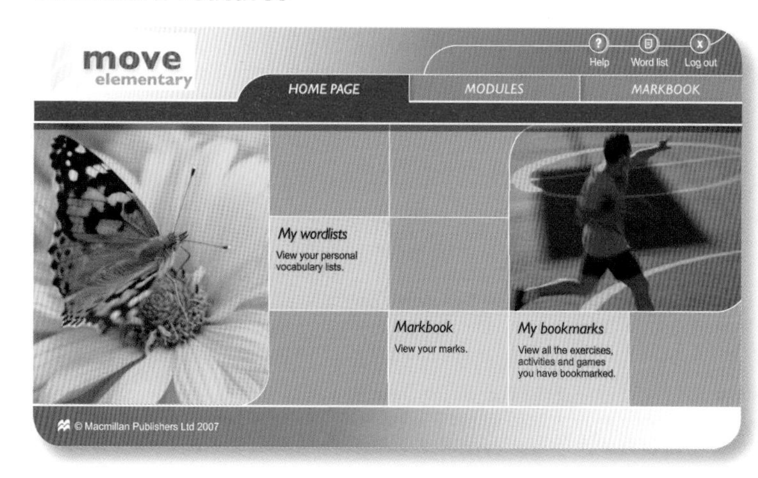

In each module:

four main units

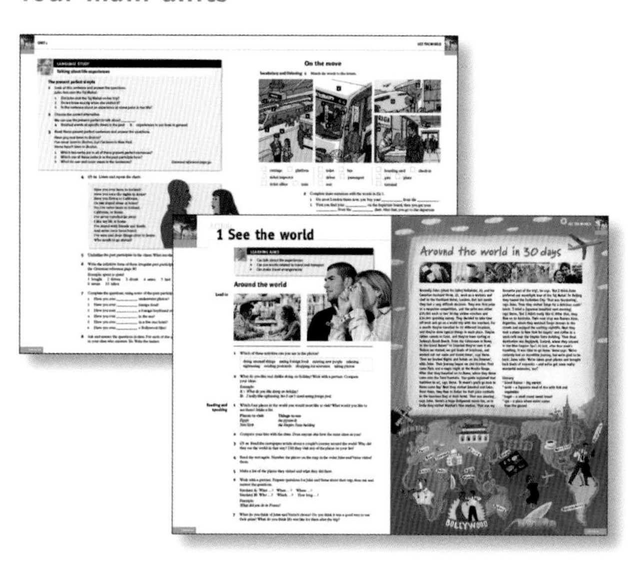

a review unit

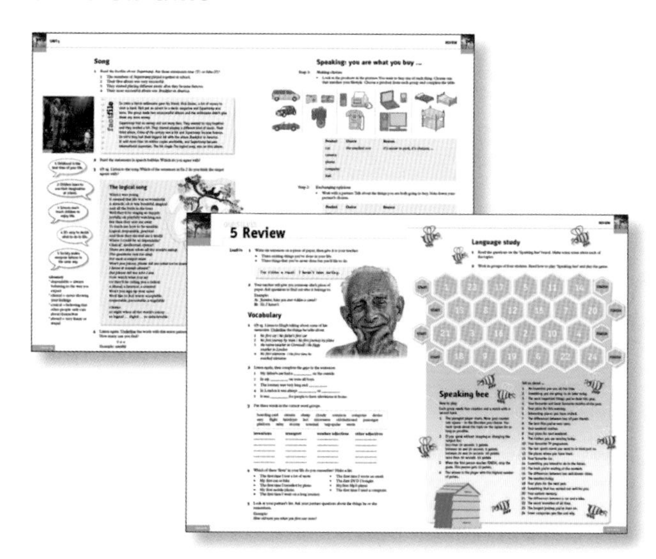

four extra practice pages

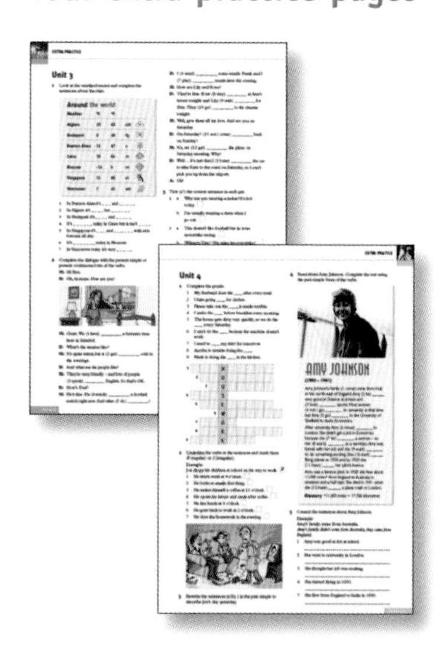

five reference pages: grammar, wordlist and listening scripts

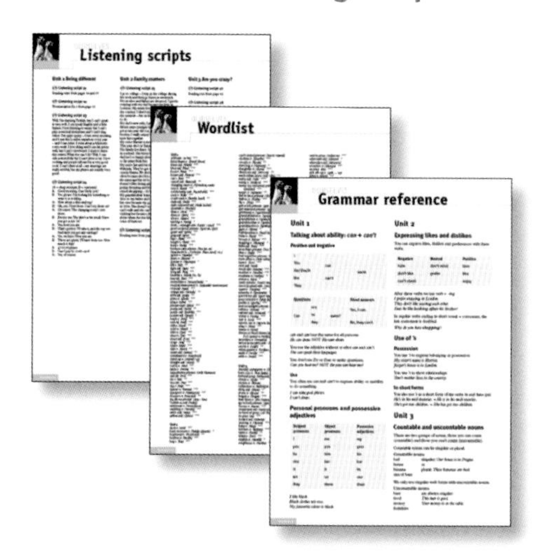

two communication activity pages

Module 1
Worldwide

nit	Topic	Language study	Vocabulary	Main skills
Home and away pages 2–5	• Visit Brighton • This is home now	• Describing places using *be* and *have got* • Articles and determiners	• Facilities in a town • Adjectives to describe places	• **Reading:** understanding main ideas • **Speaking:** expressing personal preferences; asking for and giving factual information about a place • **Listening:** understanding key information • **Pronunciation:** weak forms
Other lives pages 6–9	• Living abroad (radio programme) • My day • This is my life	• Talking about general truths (present simple)	• Verbs to talk about daily activities • Phrasal verbs to talk about daily routines	• **Listening:** understanding gist information • **Speaking:** asking and answering personal questions; giving a short personal presentation • **Reading:** understanding and transferring key information • **Writing:** note-taking for a presentation
It's a small world pages 10–13	• Staying in touch (communication) • Mobile world (using your mobile phone)	• Describing things happening now (present continuous)	• Numbers 1–100 • Telling the time	• **Listening:** extracting specific information; numbers • **Pronunciation:** *-teen* or *-ty* • **Speaking:** asking for and giving personal information; making and receiving phone calls • **Reading:** scanning a factual leaflet for specific information
This month pages 14–17	• World events (art and culture) • International line up (the London Marathon)	• Talking about frequency (adverbs of frequency)	• Countries and adjectives of nationality • Months and dates	• **Reading:** understanding specific information • **Speaking:** talking about events and dates • **Listening:** understanding specific information in dialogues

1 Home and away

LEARNING AIMS

- Can describe places using *be* and *have got*
- Can talk about town facilities
- Can express personal preferences

Lead-in

1 Which of these things are there in or near your home town? Tick (✓) the boxes.

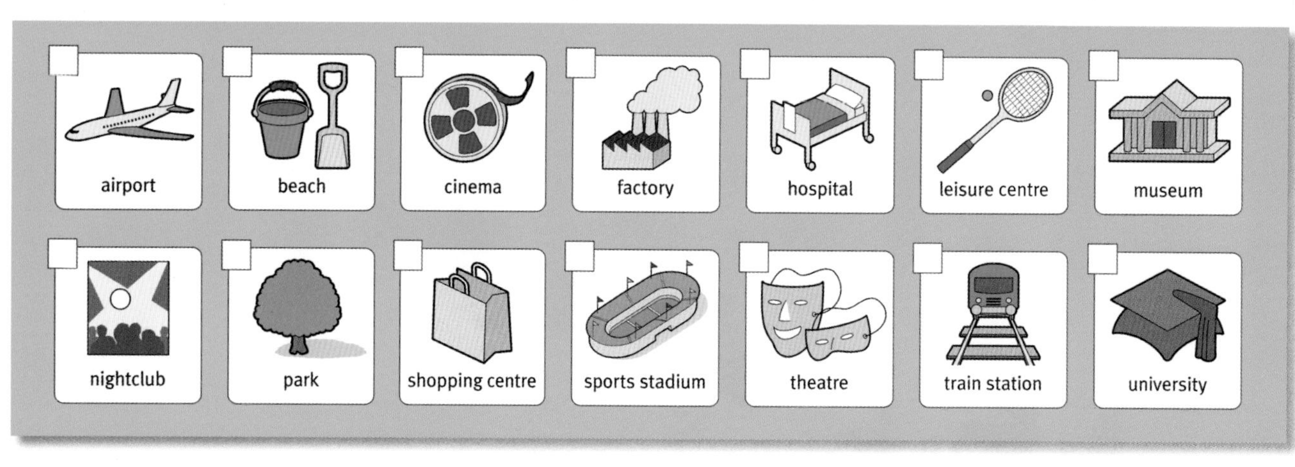

2 Work with a partner. Ask and answer questions about your home town.

Example:
A: *Is there a hospital?* **B:** *No, there isn't. / Yes, there is. It's in the city centre.*
A: *Are there any parks?* **B:** *Yes, there are lots of parks.*

Visit Brighton

Reading and vocabulary

1 **01** Read the page from a tourist guidebook about Brighton, a city in Britain, on page 3. List the places in Lead-in Ex 1 that are mentioned.

2 Complete the text with these headings.

a Entertainment b Student life c Places to see d Getting there

3 Imagine you want to study in Brighton. Tick (✓) **four** questions you want the answers for.

1 How far is Brighton from the nearest airport? ☐
2 How many universities are there? ☐
3 Are there a lot of foreign students? ☐
4 Is it an expensive place to live? ☐
5 Has Brighton got any famous buildings? ☐
6 Where are the good shops? ☐

4 Read about Brighton again and answer the questions you chose in Ex 3.

5 Find adjectives in the text which mean:

Example: full of people *busy*

1 it looks nice ____________
2 a lot of people like it ____________
3 not large ____________
4 very good ____________
5 not dangerous ____________
6 new ____________
7 not boring ____________
8 old and famous ____________

6 Use the words in Ex 5 to make true sentences about your home town.

Example: *It isn't **popular** with tourists.*

BRIGHTON

☐ ____________

An attractive city by the sea in the south of England, Brighton is popular with visitors from all over the world. There are fast trains from Brighton station to London, and Gatwick airport is only 40 km away. Brighton is a small city, but it is easy to get to.

☐ ____________

Brighton has got two universities, many good English language schools, and a famous film school. It's a truly international 'student city' with thousands of young foreign language students as well as local British students. The nightlife is good and there are many excellent restaurants, bars, pubs and nightclubs. The city is a great place for students because it isn't an expensive place to live, the people are very friendly and it's very safe too.

☐ ____________

Music is an important part of life in Brighton. There's something for everyone – from jazz to disco, and funk to reggae. The streets are busy all year. In spring there's a street theatre festival, and in summer there's an open-air cinema on the beach, and there are many open-air concerts too. Brighton marina is home to a modern leisure and shopping centre.

☐ ____________

Brighton has got a lot of interesting sights. If you've got time, visit King George IV's palace, The Royal Pavilion. It's a beautiful old building. On Sunday afternoons there are concerts there. The Brighton Museum is interesting too. Brighton's beaches, and the shops in the historic city centre, are also popular. The old Lanes area of the city has got a lot of interesting shops and cafes, and the sea is great for summer watersports.

Speaking

1 Work with a partner. You are visiting Brighton for a day. What would you like to do? Discuss your ideas.

Example: *In the morning I'd like to go to the old Lanes. In the afternoon I'd like to go to the beach, and in the evening I'd like to …*

2 What things are important for you when you choose a place to live or study? Put these things in order. 1 = very important 10 = unimportant.

a good hospital ☐ friendly people ☐ good leisure facilities ☐

good schools ☐ great shops ☐ interesting sights ☐

international restaurants ☐ lots of nightlife ☐ near the sea ☐ safe ☐

3 Compare your ideas with a partner. How similar are your lists? Tell the class.

LANGUAGE STUDY

Describing places using *be* and *have got*

1 Underline the verbs in these sentences. Which are singular (S) and which are plural (P)?

1 *Brighton is a small city.*
2 *The streets are busy all year.*
3 *There's a cinema on the beach in summer.*
4 *There are a lot of theatres in the city.*

2 Look at the sentences and complete the rules with *have got* and *has got*.

Brighton ***has got*** *two universities.* *If you****'ve got*** *time, visit King George IV's palace.*

1 With *I*, *you*, *we* and *they* we use ___________. The short form is *'ve got*.
2 With *he*, *she*, and *it* we use ___________. The short form is *'s got*.

3 Look at these sentences and answer the questions.

There isn't *a good shopping centre.* ***Is there*** *a good shopping centre?*
It ***hasn't got*** *a film school.* ***Has*** *it* ***got*** *a film school?*

1 How do we make negative sentences?
2 How do we make questions?

Grammar reference page 26

4 Look at the poster about Brighton pier. Read the questions and write the correct answer from the box.

Yes, it has.	No, it isn't.
Yes, there is.	Yes, it is.
Yes, there are.	No, there isn't.

Example: Is the pier open all year?
Yes, it is.

1 Is there a cinema on the pier?
____

2 Are there any restaurants?
____

3 Has the pier got any shops?
____

4 Is there a pub on the pier?
____

5 Is the pier new?
____

Speaking

1 Choose one place from the list or a city in your country. Make notes about it.

Ankara	Buenos Aires	Cambridge	Dubai	Krakow	Madrid	
New York	Pisa	Riyadh	Sydney	Tokyo	Venice	Xi'an

City	Size	By the sea?	Old or modern?	Attractive?	Historic sights?	Good nightlife?	Great shops?
Oxford	*small*	*no*	*old*	*yes*	*yes*	*yes*	*no*

2 Work with a partner. Ask and answer questions to guess your partner's city.

A: *Is it an attractive city?*
B: *Yes, it is.*
A: *Are there any historic sights?*
B: *Yes. The university buildings are very famous and there are two museums.*

This is home now

Listening and pronunciation

1 Work with a partner. Look at the places in the photos. What facilities do you think there are in each place?

☐ Eynsham, a village in central England

☐ York, a city in the north-east of England

☐ Barrow-in-Furness, a town in the north-west of England

2 02 Listen to three people talking about where they live. Number the places.

3 Listen again. Which sentences are about which places? Tick (✓) the correct column.

		York	Barrow	Eynsham
1	It isn't very attractive.			
2	There are some great shops.			
3	It isn't very interesting.			
4	It's by the sea.			
5	There are lots of factories.			
6	The village centre is old.			
7	It's an expensive place to live.			
8	It's got seven pubs.			
9	There aren't many foreigners.			
10	It hasn't got a cinema.			

4 Complete these sentences.

Example: I'm _a_ student at _the_ university.

1 It's _____ expensive city to live in.
2 _____ countryside near York is beautiful.
3 It's _____ large town in _____ north-west of England.
4 I live with _____ English family.
5 It's next to _____ River Thames.
6 There isn't _____ cinema.

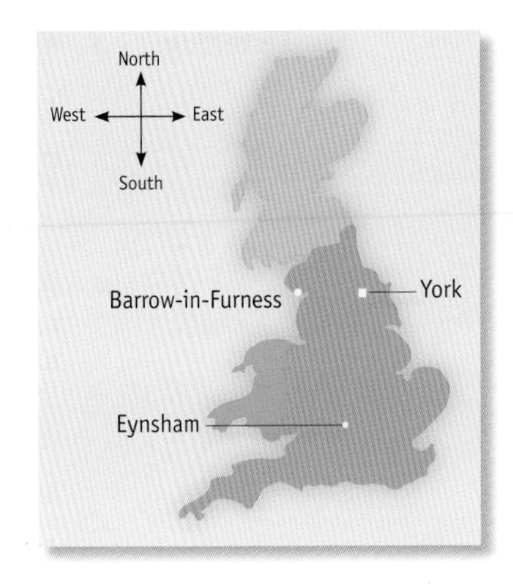

5 03 Listen and check your answers. Practise saying the sentences.

Speaking

1 Choose a town or city. You are going to persuade another student to visit it. Make notes about all the good points.

It's an old town.
It's got a great leisure centre.
There are lots of nightclubs and bars.

2 Work in pairs. Student A you are a foreign student. You are thinking of visiting student B's town. Student B you want student A to visit your town. Speak about all the good things. Use the language in the box to help you.

You must visit … Really? It's got … I see There are … Yes? That sounds interesting! Great!

3 Would you like to visit your partner's town? Tell the class something interesting about his / her town.

CD-ROM For more activities go to **Worldwide Unit 1**

WORLDWIDE

2 Other lives

LEARNING AIMS

- Can talk about general truths
- Can use phrasal verbs to talk about daily routines
- Can ask and answer personal questions

Living abroad

Lead-in

1 Work with a partner. Read these sentences. Which of them are true about life in your country? Do you know any countries they are true about? Discuss your ideas.

We eat a lot of fast food.

Most people in offices work from 9 to 5.

Most students study at universities near home.

We have a big meal at lunchtime.

We kiss people three times when we say hello.

People smoke a lot in cafes and bars.

2 Make true sentences about life in your country using the underlined verbs in Ex 1.

Listening

1 **04** Listen to part of a radio programme and choose the correct alternative.

1 It's the *beginning* / *middle* / *end* of the programme.
2 The programme is about *food* / *music* / *people's lives*.

2 **05** Listen to the next part of the programme. Match the speakers to the things they talk about. Write *S* (Sang Jin) or *A* (Annabel) in the boxes.

the language	☐	the weather	☐
food	☐	work	☐
relationships	☐	free time	☐

3 Listen again and choose the correct answers about Sang Jin and Annabel.

1 Does Sang Jin work in Korea? Yes, he does. / No, he doesn't.
2 Does he have a Korean girlfriend? Yes, he does. / No, he doesn't.
3 Does he miss his family? Yes, he does. / No, he doesn't.
4 Does Annabel come from California? Yes, she does. / No, she doesn't.
5 Does she understand Icelandic? Yes, she does. / No, she doesn't.
6 Does she speak English in her classes? Yes, she does. / No, she doesn't.

4 Work with a partner and discuss the questions.

popular magazines	radio and TV chat shows	TV reality shows

1 Think of examples in your country of the things in the box.
2 What do they tell you about people's lives?
3 Do you like them?

LANGUAGE STUDY

Talking about general truths

The present simple

1 Look at these sentences and answer the questions.

a *I **live** in Reykjavik.*
b *My friend **plays** the guitar.*
c *My girlfriend's parents **help** me a lot.*
d *I **don't come** from Iceland.*
e *She **doesn't like** Korean food.*

1 When do we use the present simple?
   a for actions happening now.
   b for things that are true all the time, and things we do repeatedly.
2 Why does the verb in sentence b end in *-s*?
3 Which of the sentences are negative?
4 When do we use *doesn't*?

2 Complete the questions and short answers.

a ___________ Annabel come from California? Yes, she ___________.
b ___________ Sang Jin live in Korea? No, he ___________.

3 How do we make questions and short answers with *I* and *you*? Choose the correct alternative.

1 *Do / Does* you speak French? No, I *don't / doesn't* .
2 *Do / Does* you come from Spain? Yes, I *do / don't* .

Grammar reference pages 26–27

4 **06** Listen and repeat the *he / she / it* forms of these verbs. Pay attention to the pronunciation of the *-s* ending.

Example: live *lives*

1	come	___________	6	live	___________
2	drink	___________	7	speak	___________
3	go	___________	8	study	___________
4	have	___________	9	watch	___________
5	kiss	___________	10	work	___________

5 Guess how to write the verb forms in Ex 4. Then check your answers in Listening script 06 on page 30.

6 Write questions for a partner using the words in the boxes.

Example:
Do you come from a big family?

come	in the evenings
drink	from a big family
go	on your own
have	abroad on holiday
live	a rest in the afternoon
play	chat shows on TV
watch	a musical instrument
work	wine with your meals

7 Work with a person in your class who you don't know well. Ask and answer your questions.

8 Tell the class about your partner.

My day

Reading and vocabulary

1 Work with a partner. Ask and answer these questions about a normal weekday in your life.

1 How long do you spend at work or at school?
2 How many hours do you sleep?
3 How much time do you spend on your own?
4 How long do you spend travelling?
5 How much time do you spend with your family?

2 Tell the class one thing about your partner.

3 Look at the photos on page 9. Check you understand these words. Which article do you think they are in?

culture hostel library medicine port pub sea ship swimsuit

4 07 Work with a partner. Student A read about William. Student B read about Ashley. Read your article carefully and complete the table.

Name	
Age	
Comes from	
Lives	
Studies	
Hobbies	

5 Work with a partner. Ask and answer questions to complete the table for the other person.

Example:
Student A: *What's Ashley's full name?*

6 Read the articles again and underline these phrasal verbs.

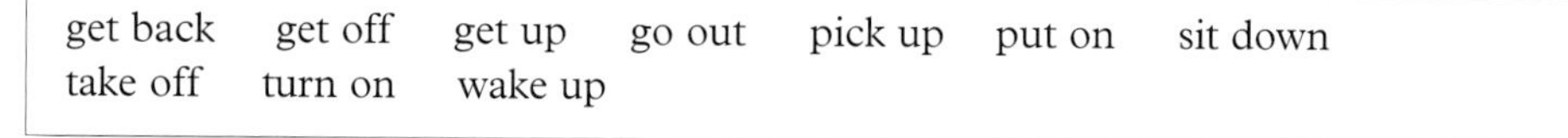

get back get off get up go out pick up put on sit down
take off turn on wake up

7 Complete these sentences with the phrasal verbs from the article.

Example: When I *wake up* early, I spend some time in bed.

1 I _____________ early because I don't want to miss breakfast.
2 _____________ your coat – it's raining!
3 I _____________ the bus at the last stop.
4 Most days, I _____________ home at about 6.30 in the evening.
5 Remember to close the door when you _____________!
6 I _____________ the computer and read my emails before breakfast.
7 If I _____________ in front of the TV late at night, I fall asleep.
8 _____________ your sunglasses in class, please!
9 I _____________ my son from school and take him to football practice.

8 Work with a partner. Think about a normal weekday in your life. Make eight sentences about your day. Six must be true and two must be false. Use as many of the phrasal verbs in Ex 6 as possible. Listen and guess which of your partner's sentences are false.

What do you do all day?

Ashley Boone, 20, student on the Semester at Sea programme

Studies 9 hours: At sea we have classes every day. There are no weekends, just port days and sea days. My favourite course is World Studies. It's about the history and culture of the countries we visit on the ship. At college back home in the United States I study Social Science.

Sleep 5 hours: I love sleeping on the ship. When I wake up in the morning I put on a swimsuit and a T-shirt and get to the dining room fast.

Me 15 minutes: There are 630 of us on the ship, and we do everything together. We even 'shower' together – we take off our T-shirts and jump into the sea. After dinner I go to the lounge and play the piano – my only time on my own in the day.

Travel 24 hours: We travel all the time – except when we get off the ship to visit the countries that we stop in.

Family 15 minutes: I spend 15 minutes every day writing to my family. I send the letters when we stop in a port – and I pick up my letters from home.

William Coulter, 22, medical student at UCL

Sleep 7 hours: My alarm clock goes off at 8.30. I turn it off and go back to sleep. Then Alex, my roommate, bangs on my door and I get up. No time for a shower!

Studies 8 hours: At 9.29 I sit down in my first class. I find it hard to think first thing. We have five hours of classes a day. Most afternoons I go to the library or study in my room. Studying medicine is a lot of work!

Travel 10 minutes: I don't travel much. I live in a student hostel and my classes are in a building down the road. In the evening I go out with friends. We walk to a pub or watch TV at a friend's house. At the weekend I go climbing. That's the only real travelling I do.

Family 30 minutes: When I get back home after class, I turn on the computer and check emails from my family and friends in Edinburgh. I go home for the weekend every two or three months. It's a long way from London to Edinburgh, and expensive too.

This is my life

Writing and speaking

1 Imagine you are a radio programme guest. You are going to prepare and give a 30 second presentation about your life. Look at Listening script 05 on page 30.

Think about your answers to these questions:

- What's great about your life?
- How do you spend your days?
- Do you have any problems?

2 Write notes for your presentation.

3 Work in groups. One person is the radio DJ. Take turns to give your presentations. Use your notes to help you speak.

CD-ROM For more activities go to **Worldwide Unit 2**

3 It's a small world

LEARNING AIMS

- Can describe things happening now
- Can ask about and tell the time
- Can make and receive phone calls

Staying in touch

Lead-in

1 Which of these means of communication do you use? Tick (✓) the boxes.

emails ☐ a mobile phone ☐ letters ☐ postcards ☐ birthday cards ☐
a chat room ☐ text messages ☐ MSN (instant messaging) ☐

2 Tell the class about yourself. Who is the most frequent communicator?

Example:
I send about ten emails a day.
I use my mobile phone about 15 or maybe 20 times a day.

Listening and vocabulary

1 **08** Listen and match these photos to two of the phone calls.

2 Listen again and choose the numbers you hear in each call.

1 0258 0471 / 0258 2471 / 8258 0471
2 11 / 12 / 20
3 14 / 40 / 44
4 19 / 90 / 99

Pronunciation

***-teen* or *-ty*?**

1 **09** Listen to each pair of numbers. Is the order correct (✓) or incorrect (✗)?

a 13 30 ✗ e 17 70 ☐
b 40 14 ☐ f 80 18 ☐
c 15 50 ☐ g 19 90 ☐
d 60 16 ☐

2 **10** Play bingo! Circle six numbers. Listen and cross out any of your six numbers that you hear. The winner is the first player with six numbers crossed out. Say 'bingo!'

11 12 13 14 15 16 17 18 19 20
21 22 23 24 25 26 27 28 29 30
40 50 60 70 80 90 100

3 Write six numbers that are important to you on a piece of paper. Swap papers with a partner. Ask your partner questions to find out what the numbers are.

Example: 45 3 9 27 12 36
Do you live at number 45?
Is 36 your lucky number?

1 one **2** two **3** three **4** four **5** five **6** six **7** seven **8** eight **9** nine **10** ten **11** eleven **12** twelve
13 thirteen **14** fourteen **15** fifteen **16** sixteen **17** seventeen **18** eighteen **19** nineteen

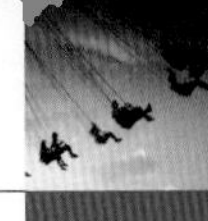

LANGUAGE STUDY

Describing things happening now

The present continuous

1 Look at these sentences from the phone calls and choose the correct alternative.

1 *He**'s coming** to pick you up.*
2 ***Are** you **watching** MTV?*
3 *Of course he **isn't working**.*
4 ***I'm** not **watching** TV!*
5 *We**'re coming** into Oxford.*
6 *What **are** you **doing**?*

1 We can use the present continuous for:
   a actions happening at the moment of speaking.
   b things that are true all the time.
2 We make the present continuous with:
   a the verb ***to be*** + the **infinitive**
   b the verb ***to be*** + the ***-ing*** **form** of the verb.

NOTE

With verbs that end in *-e* we add *-ing* but don't use the *-e*.

come → coming

Grammar reference page 27

2 Complete the email using the present continuous.

Hi Daniella,

Great to hear from you. I (1 write) _am writing_ this email now because all my housemates are busy. Pascale (2 listen) ________ to music in her room and Ben (3 have) ________ a driving lesson. His test is next week. Marek and Lucy are at the supermarket. We (4 have) ________ a barbecue in the garden and they (5 buy) ________ some more food and drink. The weather is warm and the garden (6 look) ________ great.

Hope to see you again, soon.

Best wishes,
Jenny

3 Look at the pictures and read the questions. Choose the correct answers from the box.

No, he isn't.	No, they aren't.	Yes, she is.	No, she isn't.	Yes, he is.	Yes, they are.

Example: Are they talking on the phone? *Yes, they are.*

1 Is he sitting on the beach? ____________
2 Is she walking past the cinema? ____________
3 Are they watching TV? ____________
4 Is she wearing a blue and red jacket? ____________
5 Is he wearing trainers? ____________
6 Is she looking unhappy? ____________
7 Is he holding a mobile in his hand? ____________

Speaking

1 Work with a partner. Student A turn to page 29 and look at the picture. Student B asks questions to find six differences between the picture on page 29 and this page.

Example: Student B: *Is he holding the mobile in his right hand?* Student A: *No, he isn't.*

2 Student B turn to page 32 and look at the picture of the woman. Student A asks questions to find four differences between the pictures.

20 twenty **21** twenty-one **30** thirty **40** forty **50** fifty **60** sixty **70** seventy **80** eighty **90** ninety **100** a hundred

Mobile world

Speaking and reading

1 Interview a partner using the mobile phone survey questions.

mobile phone survey

1 **Have you got a mobile phone?**
Yes ○ No, but I'd like one ○ No, I don't want one ○

2 **What make is it?**
Nokia ○ Motorola ○ Something else (What?) ____________

3 **Which mobile phone network are you with?**
Vodafone ○ T Mobile ○ Another: ____________

4 **What do you do with your mobile?**
Text friends ○ Use it for work ○ Use it in the car ○ Call friends ○
Play music ○ Send emails ○ Take photos & videos ○
Other: ____________

2 Tell the class about your partner.
Example:
Alberto's got a Nokia. He's with Vodafone, and he uses his mobile to text his friends.

mobile phone guide

To make a call from Britain to a city in another country:

- dial the international code 00
- dial the country code (see table)
- dial the city code (don't dial the first 0)
- dial the local number

Any questions?

- Call our Helpline. Dial 192
- Or visit our website: http://NTA.net
- To top up your phone call 245

City	Country code		City code	Local time → GMT (London, UK)
Cairo	20	(Egypt)	2	+ 2
Buenos Aires	54	(Argentina)	(0) 1	- 3
São Paulo	55	(Brazil)	(0) 11	- 3
Paris	33	(France)	(0) 1	+ 1
Moscow	7	(Russia)	(0) 495	+ 3
Beijing	86	(China)	(0) 10	+ 8
Tokyo	81	(Japan)	(0) 3	+ 9

Example for the Cairo number 202 415 46 12
international code 00
country code 20
city code 2
local number 415 46 12

3 11 Read the text again and answer these questions.

1 What's the number of the Helpline? __________
2 What's the number of the TopUp line? __________
3 What's the country code when you phone São Paulo? __________
4 What's the city code for Moscow when you phone from Britain? __________
5 What's the city code for Moscow when you phone from Russia? __________
6 What's the time difference between London and Tokyo? __________

Vocabulary and listening

1 Match the times in the box to the clock faces.

a quarter past four	ten to twelve	half past six	twenty-five past two
one o'clock	a quarter to nine	ten past seven	twenty to eight

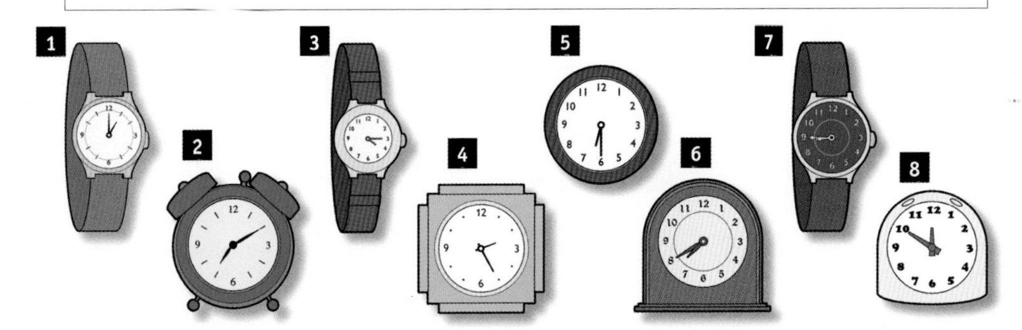

2 12 Listen and check your answers. Repeat the times.

3 13 Listen to the extracts. What's the time in these cities?

1 Sydney ________
2 Istanbul ________
3 Manchester ________
4 New York ________
5 Cape Town ________

4 Use the mobile phone guide on page 12 to prepare six questions for your partner.

Example:
It's half past six in the morning in Moscow. What's the time in London?

5 Work with a partner. Ask and answer your questions in Ex 4.

Listening and speaking

1 Read the phone call. Guess the missing phrases.

A: 1) ______________________ Hello.
B: Hello. 2) ______________________ Amy please?
A: This is Amy. 3) ______________________?
B: Hi Amy. This is Brian.
A: Brian! 4) ______________________?
B: I'm in New Zealand.
A: Wow! 5) ______________________ there?
B: It's half past seven in the morning.
A: And 6) ______________________?
B: Well, I'm having breakfast right now. 7) ______________________?
A: I'm making dinner.
B: Listen, Amy. Can you pick me up at the airport on Friday?
A: 8) ______________________. What time?
B: The plane arrives at twenty past eight in the evening.
A: OK, no problem.
B: Thanks, Amy. That's very kind of you.
A: OK. 9) ______________________ then. Bye.
B: Bye!

2 14 Listen and check your answers. Write the correct phrases.

3 Work with a partner. Student A turn to page 29. Student B turn to page 32. Read and complete your rolecards. Act out the phone call. Student A phones Student B.

CD-ROM For more activities go to **Worldwide Unit 3**

4 This month

LEARNING AIMS

- Can discuss the frequency of events
- Can use adjectives of nationality
- Can talk about events and dates

World events

Lead-in

1 Work with a partner. Find these countries on the map on page 15.

Britain	Colombia	France	Germany	India	Italy
Mexico	Morocco	New Zealand	Poland	South Korea	
Tanzania	the United States				

2 Match the photos to the events.

Wimbledon	The Academy Awards	The Cherry Blossom Festival
The Oktoberfest	Dhow countries Festival	

3 Look at the events in Ex 2. What are they? Where and when do they take place?

Reading and vocabulary

1 15 Read the World events calendar on page 15 and complete the task as fast as you can.

1 Find two sports events.
2 Find two music events.
3 Find two arts events.
4 Find a Korean event.
5 Find a British event.
6 Find a Moroccan event.

2 Read the text again and answer these questions.

1 When does the Glastonbury Festival start this year?
2 In which month does the Ironman Competition take place?
3 Which event takes place in June and July?
4 How long does the Sand Marathon last?
5 When does the Rio Carnival finish?

3 Underline the months in the text. Then complete this list with the months in order.

1st: January	5th: M_________	9th: September
2nd: F_________	6th: J _________	10th: October
3rd: M_________	7th: J_________	11th: November
4th: A_________	8th: August	12th: December

4 Work with a partner. Ask and answer questions about the months.

Example:
Which is the sixth month? Which month comes after July?

1st first	2nd second	3rd third	4th fourth	5th fifth	6th sixth	7th seventh	8th eighth
9th ninth	10th tenth	11th eleventh	12th twelfth	13th thirteenth	14th fourteenth		

World events calendar

1 **Rio Carnival Brazil (Rio de Janeiro) 17th–20th February** The world famous Brazilian carnival takes place in Rio de Janeiro every year. Thousands of samba dancers and bands fill the streets with music and colourful costumes for four days.

2 **Ironman Competition New Zealand (Taupo) 4th March** Taupo is the home of this 'Ironman' triathlon qualifying race (swimming, cycling and running). It takes place on 4th March this year. There are big money prizes. Up to 1,500 people take part, usually half of them from overseas.

3 **Sand Marathon Morocco (Ouarzazate) 7th–18th April** This long race across sand takes place near Ouarzazate from 7th–18th April. The marathon course is 150 miles (240km) long and the race lasts for a week.

4 **Seoul Cartoon and Animation Festival South Korea (Seoul) 24th–28th May** This International Festival of animated feature films, short films, TV films, and adverts, takes place in the South Korean capital, Seoul, in May.

5 **Glastonbury Festival Britain (Glastonbury) 21st–23rd June** This rock music festival takes place in June near the British town of Glastonbury. People come from all over the world to camp and listen to the different bands.

6 **Medellín Poetry Festival Colombia (Medellín) 24th June–2nd July** Thousands of people go to Medellín's International Poetry Festival. It takes place at different places around the city over nine days.

Vocabulary and speaking

1 **16** Listen and complete the dates you hear.

1	______ April	4	______ October	7	______ November
2	______ March	5	______ January	8	______ May
3	______ June	6	______ July		

2 Work with a partner. Tell your partner about four dates that are important to you.
Example: *My birthday is on 26th April.*

NOTE

We say *the 26th of April*, but we write *26th April.*

3 Work with a partner. You are going to ask and answer questions about other events. Student A turn to page 29. Student B turn to page 32. Follow the instructions.

4 Work with a partner and discuss these questions.

1 Would you like to attend any of the events in Ex 3?
2 What kind of events do you enjoy?

15th fifteenth **16th** sixteenth **17th** seventeenth **18th** eighteenth **19th** nineteenth **20th** twentieth **21st** twenty-first **30th** thirtieth **31st** thirty-first

INTERNATIONAL

line up

More than 90,000 runners from 56 different countries want to run in the Flora London Marathon next April. European countries are at the top of the list with 422 French runners followed by 345 Germans, 303 North Americans, 279 Italians and over 200 Spanish athletes. Competitors come from far and wide. There are 41 Japanese runners on the list as well as 43 Australians. The favourites to win the men's race are Kenyans Limo and Lel. In the women's race the favourites are Romanian Dita-Tomescu and American Deena Kastor. Thousands of British athletes train all year to compete. Others wear funny costumes to make money for charities.

International line up

Vocabulary and pronunciation

1 Read about the London Marathon. Find the nationality words and complete the table.

Country	Nationality	Country	Nationality
Australia	____________	Japan	____________
Britain	____________	Kenya	____________
France	____________	Romania	____________
Germany	____________	Spain	____________
Italy	____________	the United States (of America)	____________

2 **17** Listen and underline the stressed syllable in the words in Ex 1. In which two country and nationality pairs is the stress different?

Listening

1 **18** Listen to two people talking about the marathon. Write *Wendy* or *Krishnan* to complete the sentences.

1 ____________ is watching the race.
2 ____________ is running in the race.
3 ____________ is nervous.
4 ____________ is having fun.

2 Listen again Are these sentences true (T) or false (F)?

1 It's Wendy's second marathon. ☐
2 She's wearing a banana costume. ☐
3 She goes running every evening. ☐
4 Krishnan is watching the race on television. ☐
5 He doesn't like running. ☐
6 He doesn't want to watch the race next year. ☐

LANGUAGE STUDY

Talking about frequency

1 Look at these sentences from the interviews and choose the correct alternative.

I'm always nervous before the race.
I never go running.
I sometimes run in the evenings.
I hardly ever come to London.
I usually watch the marathon on television.
We often go running together at weekends.

1 Which is the tense in all the sentences? present simple / present continuous
2 What do they describe? things that are always true / routines and habits

2 Frequency words describe how often we do something. Underline the frequency words in the sentences in Ex 1.

3 Write the frequency words in order, depending on their meaning.

100% of the time ________
90% of the time ________
70% of the time ________
50% of the time ________
5% of the time ________
0% of the time ________

4 Look at the sentences again and complete the rules.

1 We put frequency words ______ the verb *be*. **a** before **b** after
2 We put frequency words ______ all other verbs. **a** before **b** after

Grammar reference page 27

Speaking and writing

1 Complete this survey about healthy habits with your answers.

HEALTHY HABITS

How often do you ...

	YOU	YOUR PARTNER
1 ... exercise for more than half an hour?	________	________
2 ... walk or cycle to school or work?	________	________
3 ... eat sweets and chocolate between meals?	________	________
4 ... eat fresh fruit and vegetables with your meals?	________	________
5 ... stay up late at the weekends?	________	________
6 ... drink alcohol with your meals?	________	________
7 ... drink coffee as soon as you wake up?	________	________
8 ... feel bad about eating too much?	________	________

1 = never 2 = hardly ever 3 = sometimes 4 = often 5 = usually 6 = always

2 Work with a partner. Interview your partner and complete his / her survey answers.

3 How healthy is your partner? Write a health report. Start like this:

Example: *Paula is quite healthy. She usually exercises for more than half an hour every day, and she sometimes exercises for more than an hour.*

CD-ROM For more activities go to **Worldwide Unit 4**

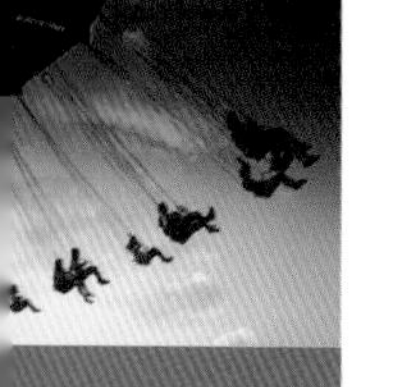

5 Review

Lead-in **1** How international are your tastes? Work with a partner. Talk about your likes and dislikes.

beer	cars	chocolate	clothes	films	food	music	perfume	wine

Example:
A: *I like English beer.*
B: *I like German cars.*
B: *I don't. I like Czech beer.*
A: *So do I.*

Language study

1 Look at the people in the picture. What are they doing?

2 19 Listen. Which people in the picture are speaking? What do they want to do?

3 Listen again and complete these sentences from the dialogues.

Dialogue 1

1 ______________________ any good restaurants near here?
2 What kind of food ______________________?
3 ______________________ far? No, ______________________.

Dialogue 2

4 What ______________________ here?
5 ______________________ his birthday on ______________________.
6 ______________________ this CD? No, ______________________.

4 Check your answers in Listening script 19 on page 31.

5 Complete the list of words to describe how often we do something.

0% n__________
5% h__________ e__________
50% s__________
70% o__________
90% u__________
100% a__________

6 Work with a partner. Make five true and one false sentence about yourself using the frequency words. Guess your partner's false sentence.

Vocabulary

colours

Blue | Red

1 Work in teams. You are going to race each other. Your teacher is going to give you a topic card. The first team to write ten words on their card wins a point. When all the topic cards are completed the team with the most points is the winner.

Topics: adjectives to describe places colours common verbs countries languages months phrasal verbs town facilities

2 Use the words in Ex 1 to make 80 small cards. Put the cards face down on the correct squares of the 'Wordwheel' game.

3 Play in teams of two. Read how to play 'Wordwheel' and play the game.

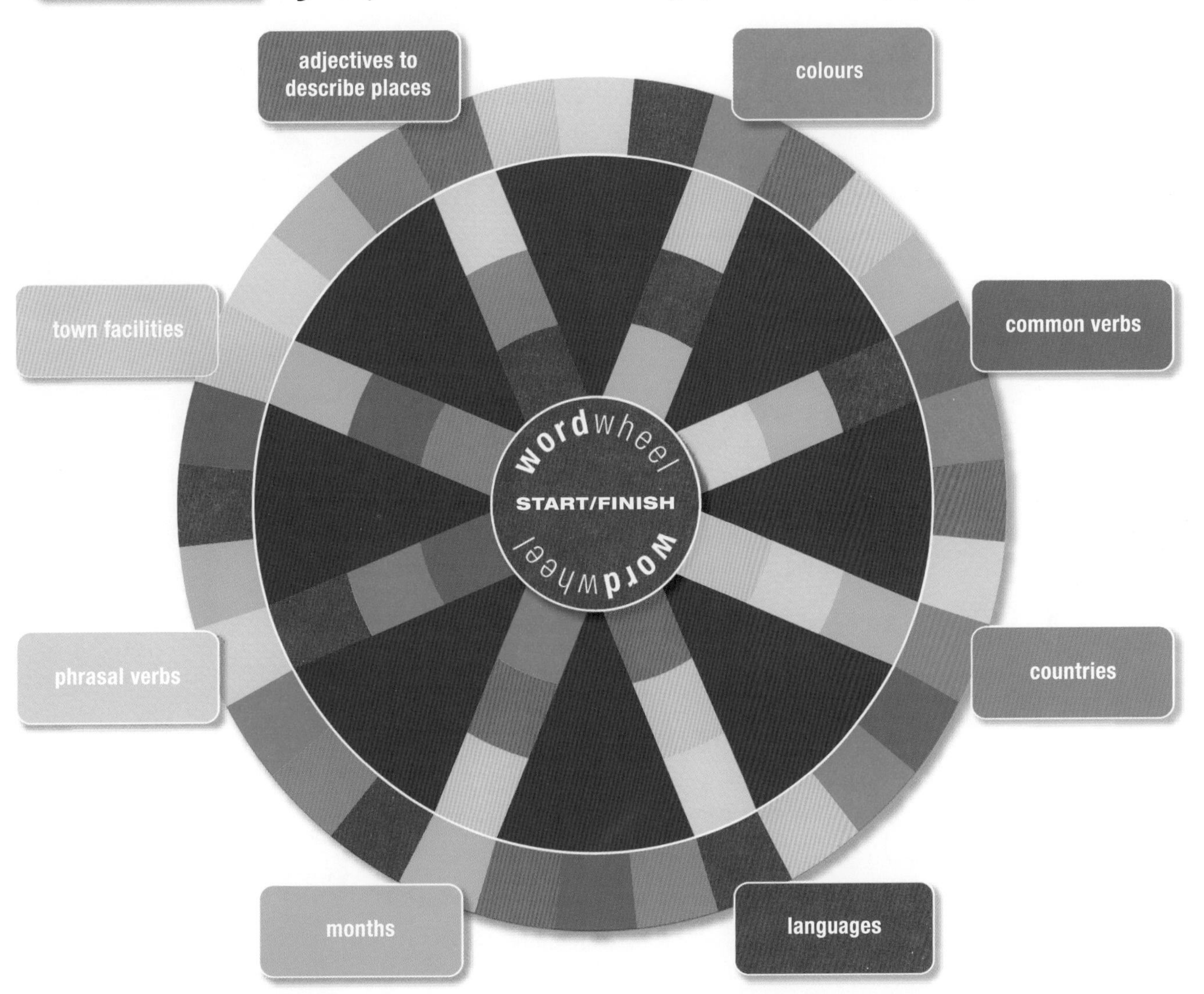

HOW TO PLAY

1 The team with the youngest player starts. Throw the dice and move your counter. You can move in any direction around the board.

2 When you land on a 'topic' square, one player in the team takes a card. It's a secret. The player has 30 seconds to help the other player in the team guess the word on the card. Don't say or write the word.

3 There are four ways to help your partner guess your word. You can:

- **Mime the word**
- **Draw the word**
- **Explain the word:** *It's the nationality of a person from Spain.*
- **Make a sentence with the word,** but don't say the word, say 'beep'.
  Ronaldinho plays for a ... beep ... football team.

4 If the other player guesses the word in time, then the team keeps the card and plays again.
If not, the player returns the card to the bottom of the cards and it's the next team's turn.

5 The first team to collect a card from each topic and arrive at the 'finish' box is the winner.

Song

1 Read the factfile about Katie Melua. Complete these sentences with the correct alternative.

1	Katie Melua is from ___.	a Moscow	b Georgia	c Belfast
2	She likes ___.	a doctors	b swimming	c acting
3	Her TV talent show prize is for ___.	a writing songs	b dancing	c singing
4	*Crawling up a hill* is from her ___ album.	a first	b second	c third

factfile

1984	Katie is born in Tbilisi in Georgia (part of the former USSR).
1987–88	Katie's family moves to Moscow in Russia.
1988–93	Katie's family moves back to Georgia. She learns to swim in the Black Sea. She still loves swimming!
1993–98	Katie's father gets a job as a doctor in Belfast, Northern Ireland.
1998	Her family moves to London. Katie starts at a new school (her seventh!) called the Brit School. It's a special school for singers and actors.
1999	Katie wins a TV talent show for singing.
2003	Katie releases her first album called *Call off the search*. The song *Crawling up a hill* comes from this album.

2 What do you think the song *Crawling up a hill* is about? Discuss your ideas in pairs.

- travelling by train
- the singer's life
- the singer having a walk
- living in the country

3 20 Listen to and read the song. What is it about? Were you right?

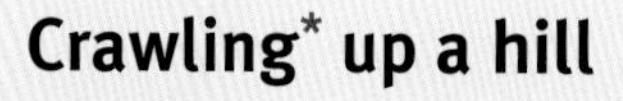

Crawling* up a hill

Every morning 'bout half past eight,
My Mamma wakes me says
"Don't be late",
Get to the office, tryin' to concentrate,
My life is just a slow train crawling up a hill.

So I stop one day to figure it out,
I'll quit* my job without a shadow of a doubt*,
To sing the blues* that I know about,
My life is just a slow train crawling up a hill.

Minute after minute,
Second after second,
Hour after hour goes by,
Working for a rich girl,
Staying just a poor girl,
Never stop to wonder why.

So here I am in London town,
A better scene I'm gonna be around,
The kind of music that won't bring me down,
My life is just a slow train crawling up a hill.

Glossary

* to crawl = to move very slowly
* to quit = to leave
* without a shadow of a doubt = certainly
* blues = sad songs

4 Are these statements about the person in the song true (T) or false (F)?

1 She lives with her mother. ☐
2 She works in an office. ☐
3 Her boss is a man. ☐
4 She wants to leave her job. ☐
5 She wants to be a singer. ☐
6 She's waiting for a train. ☐

5 Complete these sentences to make them true for you.

1 First thing in the morning, I usually hear …
2 When I leave the house, I often feel …
3 Just before I go to bed, I …
4 I sometimes want to …

6 Work with a partner. Don't show each other your sentences. Guess your partner's answers.

Example:
A: *Do you hear the alarm clock first thing in the morning?*
B: *Yes, I do.*

Speaking: a roleplay

1 Work with a partner. You are going to prepare a conversation. You can be yourselves or invent details about yourself.

Step 1: **Getting ready**
Decide which conversation you'd like to prepare:

A phonecall from a bus station. One person wants to be picked up when the bus arrives.

A conversation in a pub. You meet someone attractive and you'd like to ask them out for a meal.

Step 2: **Setting the scene**
Use these rolecards to help you prepare the conversation.

Rolecard

Phonecall

Student A
Answer the phone and say your phone number. Ask what time Student B is arriving and where.

Student B
Say who you are, where you are travelling from, and what time your bus arrives. Ask to be picked up.

Rolecard

Meeting someone

Student A
Introduce yourself. Ask about Student B: name, country, where they live, their favourite food. Suggest going somewhere to eat.

Student B
Reply to Student A's questions. Ask Student A about what they do and their favourite place. Ask what type of food they like.

Step 3: **The roleplay**
Present your roleplay to the class. Use the phrases in the boxes to help you.

Hello, this is 07917845 …
I'm coming from …
What time are you arriving at …?
Can you pick me up at …?

Is it OK if I sit here?
Of course.
Would you like to go and eat something?
I like Italian food. How about you?
There's a restaurant near here. It's called …

2 Vote for the best roleplay.

Extra practice

Unit 1

1 Complete these signs for places in a town.

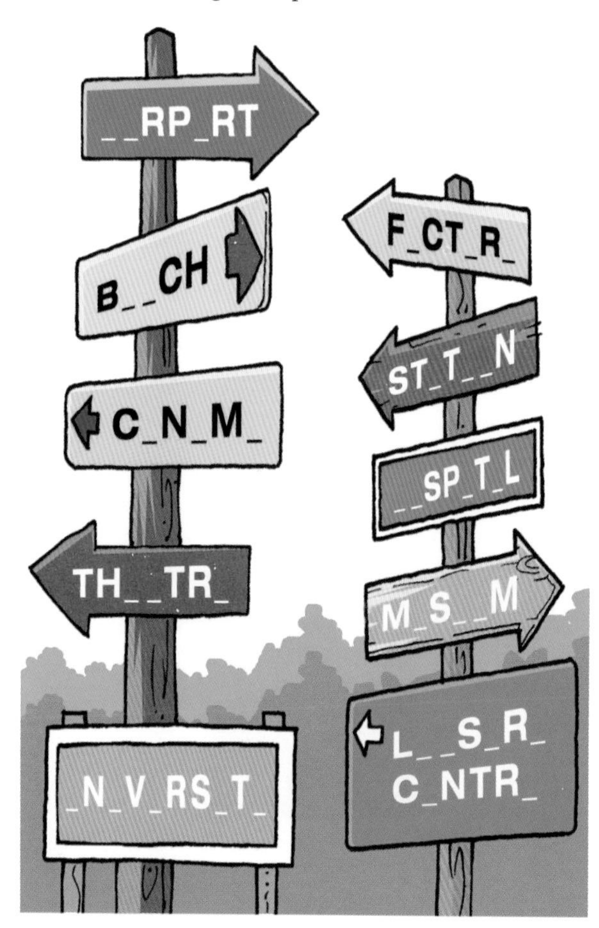

2 Write the long forms of these sentences.

Example:
Where's the museum?
Where is the museum?

1 There's an Indian restaurant here.

____

2 I'm Spanish.

____

3 My brother's got a house in Brighton.

____

4 It's got a big park.

____

5 We're from Syria.

____

6 They've got two children.

____

7 The factory isn't old.

____

8 His wife's Japanese.

____

3 Complete the text. Use the correct form of *be*, *there is / are*, and *have got*.

Shyamji Bhatnagar __*is*__ from the north of India. His wife, Alisa, (1) ____ from London. They' (2) ____ one son, Bhanu. He' (3) ____ five years old and he isn't Indian or British, he' (4) ____ American. Shyamji and Alisa's home (5) ____ now in New York. They (6) ____ yoga teachers and they've got a yoga centre near New York. The centre (7) ____ in a small town in a big old building. (8) ____ ____ more than 100 pupils in the centre and it' (9) ____ very popular. Bhanu's school (10) ____ in the same town. It (11) ____ a big school. (12) ____ ____ only 20 pupils in the school and (13) ____ ____ three teachers. Bhanu (14) ____ ____ lots of friends there and he' (15) ____ very happy.

4 Write true answers about you, your home town and your school.

Example:
Are you Italian? *No, I'm not.*

1 Are you busy in the evenings?

____

2 Are there a lot of tourists in your home town?

____

3 Is it far from your home town to an airport?

____

4 Has your home town got a good leisure centre?

____

5 Is your school in Britain?

____

6 Are there many students in your class?

____

7 Is there a computer in your classroom?

____

8 Are your lessons in the morning?

____

Unit 2

1 Complete these sentences with the correct form of the verbs in the box.

go have miss live speak study

1 Kate ____________ politics at university.
2 She ____________ a boyfriend called Jack.
3 Jack ____________ in the centre of Moscow.
4 He ____________ Russian really well now.
5 Kate ____________ Jack when he's in Moscow.
6 Jack ____________ to Britain once a month.

2 Look at the grid and complete the sentences.

Do you ... ?	Jack	Kate
speak a foreign language	✓	✗
live in a big city	✓	✗
listen to the radio	✓	✗
watch chat shows on TV	✗	✓
play a musical instrument	✗	✓
travel abroad a lot	✓	✗

1 Kate ____________ a foreign language.
2 Jack ____________ in a big city, but Kate ____________.
3 Jack ____________ to the radio and Kate ____________ chat shows on TV.
4 Kate ____________ the piano, but Jack ____________ a musical instrument.
5 Kate ____________ abroad a lot.

3 Write true sentences about yourself. Use the phrases in Ex 2.

4 Choose the correct alternative.

1 I don't want to go *up* / *off* / *out* tonight, I want to watch TV at home.
2 You look tired, why don't you sit *up* / *on* / *down*?
3 I'm always tired when I wake *off* / *out* / *up*.
4 At which station do you get *out* / *off* / *up* the train?
5 My girlfriend picks me *off* / *on* / *up* from work in the evening.
6 I'm hot. I don't want to put *on* / *about* / *up* my coat.
7 It's dark in here, turn *about* / *off* / *on* the light.
8 Please take *off* / *on* / *up* your shoes before entering the building.

5 Read about Alberto and write questions for the answers.

Alberto Rossi is from Italy. He studies English at a school in York and he lives with an English family in a small village not far from the city. The village is about five miles from the language school. Like most students Alberto goes to class by bus. He has four hours of classes in the morning and in the afternoon he plays football or goes running near the river Ouse. Alberto likes his host family – the Mayfields – a lot. His host mother, Sara, is a doctor, and her husband, Jeff, teaches at the university. They've got four children – two girls and two boys. They all like Alberto a lot.

Example: *Where does Alberto come from?* From Italy.

1 ________________________________?
At a school in York.

2 ________________________________?
By bus.

3 ________________________________?
No, he doesn't. He only has classes in the morning.

4 ________________________________?
He plays football or goes running.

5 ________________________________?
At the university.

6 Write a similar text about someone you know.

Unit 3

1 Write the numbers.

a	1	*one*	j	14	______
b	2	______	k	15	______
c	3	______	l	16	______
d	4	______	m	100	______
e	5	______	n	20	______
f	6	______	o	31	______
g	11	______	p	48	______
h	12	______	q	50	______
i	13	______	r	67	______

2 Write the times.

1 It's *twenty to twelve.*

2 ______

3 ______

4 ______

5 ______

6 ______

3 Rearrange these words to make present continuous sentences.

Example:
lunch / they / the / are / airport / at / having
They are having lunch at the airport.

1 coat / are / a / wearing / why / you / ?

______

2 to each other / sisters / talking / not / my / are

______

3 today / restaurant / Jenny / is / the / working / at / ?

______

4 you / TV channel / watching / are / which / ?

______

5 not / computer / using / his / is / Paul / at the moment

______

4 Look carefully at the picture of David and Julie. Write six sentences about what's happening. Use the words in the box.

hold sit stand read talk wait

______

______

______

______

______

______

5 Put the telephone call in the correct order.

a How about half-past seven?
b 0217 634266. Hello? *1*
c Half past seven? That sounds great.
d All right. Bye.
e Chinese? Er … yes, I'd love to. What time?
f Hi Ruth, this is Stephen.
g I'm fine. Listen, Ruth would you like to go out to a Chinese restaurant tonight?
h Oh, hi Stephen. How are you?
i Good. OK then. See you later.
j Bye.

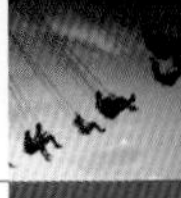

Unit 4

1 Look at the table and complete the sentences with countries or nationalities.

ATHENS 2004

Gold Medal Winners

Sport	Event		Country	Winner
Athletics	50km walk	men	POL	Robert KORZENIOWSKI
Athletics	800m	women	GBR	Kelly HOLMES
Athletics	marathon	men	ITA	Stefano BALDINI
Athletics	marathon	women	JAP	Mizuki NOGUCHI
Sailing		women	FRA	Faustine MERRET
Swimming	200m freestyle	men	AUS	Ian THORPE
Volleyball		men	BRA	team event

1 The winner of the men's marathon was an __________ athlete.
2 Kelly Holmes isn't American. She's a __________ runner.
3 The 200m freestyle swimming champion was from __________.
4 The __________ team won the gold in volleyball.
5 The women's marathon winner was from __________.
6 The winner of the 50km walk was from __________.
7 Faustine Merret is a __________ sailor.

2 Write these dates. Make sure you remember how to say them.

Example:
Christmas Day *25th December.*

1 last Friday __________
2 your birthday __________
3 New Year's Day __________
4 today __________
5 next Monday __________
6 April Fool's Day __________

3 Rearrange these words to make sentences.

1 to / we / go out / a restaurant / hardly ever
____
2 my / to concerts / with / never / boyfriend / I / go
____
3 breakfast / for a run / goes / before / always / Jan
____
4 the / it / rains / Wimbledon / often / during / tennis tournament
____
5 in a tent / the Festival / sleep / they / at / sometimes
____
6 race / runners / before / are / a / nervous / often
____

4 Add a frequency word to make these sentences true for you.

Example:
I walk to work.
I *sometimes* walk to work.

1 I feel tired in the morning when I wake up.
____
2 I turn off the lights when I leave a room.
____
3 I go out with my friends on Friday and Saturday evenings.
____
4 I get up in the morning in a good mood.
____
5 I sit down when I talk on the phone.
____
6 I take off my shoes before I go into a house.
____

5 Answer these questions truthfully. Use a frequency word in each answer.

Example:
When do you do your English homework?
I sometimes do it on the bus home.

1 Where do you go on holiday?
____
2 What do you do in the evening after dinner?
____
3 What's the last thing you do at night?
____
4 What do you have for breakfast?
____
5 How often do you go to the cinema?
____

WORLDWIDE

Grammar reference

Unit 1

Describing places using *be* and *have got*

be

Positive and negative

I	'm (am) 'm not	
He She It	's (is) isn't	famous. beautiful.
We You They	're (are) aren't	

Questions			**Short Answers**	
Is	he she it	famous?	Yes, he is. Yes, she is. Yes, it is.	No, he isn't. No, she isn't. No, it isn't.

Are	you we they	small?	Yes, I am. No, I'm not. Yes, we are. No, we aren't. Yes, they are. No, they aren't.

there is / are

You can use *there* + the verb *be* to describe places.

There isn't a cinema in the town centre.
There are a lot of parks.
'Are there lots of restaurants?' 'Yes there are.'

have got

Positive and negative

I You We They	've (have) haven't	got	a large house. a sister.
He She It	's (has) hasn't		

Questions				**Short Answers**	
Have	you we they	got	a large house?	Yes, I have.	No, they haven't.
Has	he she it			Yes, she has.	No, it hasn't.

Use

You use *have got:*

to talk about the things in a place
Brighton has got two universities.

to talk about possession
I've got a large house.

Unit 2

Talking about general truths

Present simple

Positive and negative

I You We They	live don't live	in Britain.
He She It	lives doesn't live	

Questions			**Short Answers**		
Do	I you we they	live in Korea?	Yes, No,	I we they	do. don't.
Does	he she it		Yes, No,	he she it	does. doesn't.

Spelling: *he / she / it* form

+ *-s*
With *he / she* and *it*, most verbs add *-s* to the infinitive form:
live → lives   *speak → speaks*   *play → plays*

+ *-es*
Verbs that end in *-s*, *-sh*, *-ch*
kiss → kisses   *wash → washes*   *watch → watches*

+ *-ies*
Verbs that end in consonant + *-y*
study → studies

Some verbs are irregular.
have → has   *do → does*   *go → goes*

Use

You use the present simple:

to talk about things that are true all the time:
I live in New Zealand.   She doesn't come from Korea.

to talk about things we do repeatedly:
Her classes begin at 7 o'clock.
He doesn't travel by bus. He comes by car.

Unit 3

Describing things happening now

Present continuous

Positive and negative		
I	'm (am) 'm not	
You We They	're (are) aren't	working. watching TV.
He She It	's (is) isn't	

Questions			
	am	I	
What	are	you we they	doing?
	is	he she it	

For *yes / no* question and short answer forms see *be* (page 26).

Spelling: present participle (*-ing* form)

Most verbs add *-ing* to the infinitive:
work → working   *do → doing*   *go → going*

Verbs ending with consonant + *-e*:
come → coming   *write → writing*   *live → living*

Verbs with consonant + short vowel + consonant:
sit → sitting   *get → getting*

Use

You can use the present continuous for actions happening at the moment of speaking.
Are you watching TV? Yes, I am.
They aren't watching a film.

Unit 4

Talking about frequency

Adverbs of frequency

You use adverbs of frequency to say *how often* you do something.

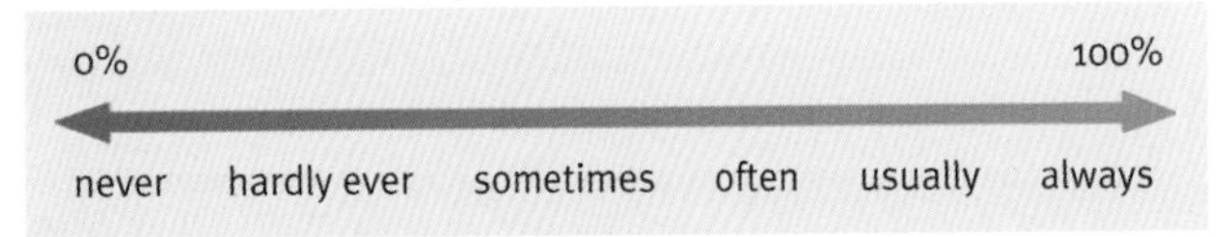

Adverbs of frequency usually go between the subject and the verb:
***I** hardly ever **go** running.*
***They** never **drink** alcohol.*

With the verb ***to be*** the adverb of frequency goes after the verb:
***We're sometimes** nervous.*
***It's always** hot in the summer.*

Prepositions of time

in	+ time	*My birthday is **in** July.*
	+ time of day	*I go running **in** the morning / afternoon / evening.* ***But note: at** night*
at	+ time	*The class starts **at** nine o'clock.*
on	+ date	*The tour starts **on** 1st February.*
	+ day	*My class is **on** Monday.*
from ... **to ...**	(start) (finish)	*Our class is **from** nine to ten.* *The festival takes place **from** 22nd **to** 24th June.*

WORLDWIDE

Wordlist

*** the 2,500 most common English words, ** very common words, * fairly common words

Unit 1

airport *n* /ˈeəˌpɔːt/ ***
attractive *adj* /əˈtræktɪv/ ***
beach *n* /biːtʃ/ ***
boring *adj* /ˈbɔːrɪŋ/ **
busy *adj* /ˈbɪzi/ ***
cinema *n* /ˈsɪnəmə/ **
dangerous *adj* /ˈdeɪndʒərəs/ ***
entertainment *n* /ˌentəˈteɪnmənt/ *
excellent *adj* /ˈeksələnt/ ***
expensive *adj* /ɪkˈspensɪv/ ***
factory *n* /ˈfæktri/ ***
famous *adj* /ˈfeɪməs/ ***
foreign *adj* /ˈfɒrɪn/ ***
friendly *adj* /ˈfrendli/ ***
great *adj* /greɪt/ ***
historic *adj* /hɪˈstɒrɪk/ **
hospital *n* /ˈhɒspɪtl/ ***
interesting *adj* /ˈɪntrəstɪŋ/ ***
international *adj* /ˌɪntəˈnæʃnəl/ ***
language *n* /ˈlæŋgwɪdʒ/ ***
large *adj* /lɑːdʒ/ ***
leisure centre *n* /ˈleʒə ˌsentə/
leisure facilities *n* /ˈleʒə fəˌsɪlətiz/
modern *adj* /ˈmɒdən/ ***
museum *n* /mjuːˈziːəm/ ***
near *prep* /nɪə/ ***
new *adj* /njuː/ ***
nightclub *n* /ˈnaɪtˌklʌb/
nightlife *n* /ˈnaɪtˌlaɪf/
old *adj* /əʊld/ ***
park *n* /pɑːk/ ***
pier *n* /pɪə/ *
popular *adj* /ˈpɒpjʊlə/ ***
pub *n* /pʌb/ ***
restaurant *n* /ˈrestərɒnt/ ***
safe *adj* /seɪf/ ***
sea *n* /siː/ ***
shopping centre *n* /ˈʃɒpɪŋ ˌsentə/
sight *n* /saɪt/ ***
small *adj* /smɔːl/ ***
sports stadium *n* /ˈspɔːts ˌsteɪdiəm/
theatre *n* /ˈθɪətə/ ***
train station *n* /ˈtreɪn ˌsteɪʃn/
university *n* /ˌjuːnɪˈvɜːsəti/ ***

Unit 2

close *v* /kləʊz/ ***
come (from) *v* /ˈkʌm (frəm)/ ***
culture *n* /ˈkʌltʃə/ ***
drink *n, v* /drɪŋk/ ***
eat *v* /iːt/ ***
get back *v* /ˌget ˈbæk/
get off *v* /ˌget ˈɒf/
get up *v* /ˌget ˈʌp/
go off *v* /ˌgəʊ ˈɒf/
go out *v* /ˌgəʊ ˈaʊt/
go *v* /gəʊ/ ***
have *v* /hæv/ ***
hostel *n* /ˈhɒstəl/
Iceland *n* /ˈaɪslənd/
kiss *v* /kɪs/ ***
Korean *adj* /kəˈriːən/
library *n* /ˈlaɪbrəri/ ***
live *v* /lɪv/ ***
medicine *n* /ˈmedsn/ ***
miss *v* /mɪs/ ***
New Zealander *adj* /ˌnjuː ˈziːləndə/
pick up *v* /ˌpɪk ˈʌp/
port *n* /pɔːt/ ***
put on *v* /ˌpʊt ˈɒn/
rain(ing) *v* /reɪn(ɪŋ)/ ***
read *v* /riːd/ ***
send *v* /send/ ***
ship *n* /ʃɪp/ ***
sit (down) *v* /ˌsɪt (ˈdaʊn)/ ***
smoke *v* /sməʊk/ **
speak *v* /spiːk/ ***
spend *v* /spend/ ***
study *v* /ˈstʌdi/ ***
swimsuit *n* /ˈswɪmsuːt/
take off *v* /ˌteɪk ˈɒf/
take *v* /teɪk/ ***
travel *v* /ˈtrævl/ ***
turn off *v* /ˌtɜːn ˈɒf/
turn on *v* /ˌtɜːn ˈɒn/
understand *v* /ˌʌndəˈstænd/ ***
wake up *v* /ˌweɪk ˈʌp/
want *v* /wɒnt/ ***
watch *v* /wɒtʃ/ ***
work *v* /wɜːk/ ***

Unit 3

one /wʌn/ ***
two /tuː/ ***
three /θriː/
four /fɔː/
five /faɪv/
six /sɪks/
seven /ˈsevn/
eight /eɪt/
nine /naɪn/
ten /ten/
eleven /ɪˈlevn/
twelve /twelv/
thirteen /ˌθɜːˈtiːn/
fourteen /ˌfɔːˈtiːn/
fifteen /ˌfɪfˈtiːn/
sixteen /ˌsɪksˈtiːn/
seventeen /ˌsevnˈtiːn/
eighteen /ˌeɪˈtiːn/
nineteen /ˌnaɪnˈtiːn/
twenty /ˈtwenti/
twenty-one /ˌtwenti ˈwʌn/
twenty-two /ˌtwenti ˈtuː/
twenty-three /ˌtwenti ˈθriː/
twenty-four /ˌtwenti ˈfɔː/
twenty-five /ˌtwenti ˈfaɪv/
twenty-six /ˌtwenti ˈsɪks/
twenty-seven /ˌtwenti ˈsevn/
twenty-eight /ˌtwenti ˈeɪt/
twenty-nine /ˌtwenti ˈnaɪn/
thirty /ˈθɜːti/
forty /ˈfɔːti/
fifty /ˈfɪfti/
sixty /ˈsɪksti/
seventy /ˈsevnti/
eighty /ˈeɪti/
ninety /ˈnaɪnti/
a hundred /ə ˈhʌndrəd/
(five) past ... *phrase* /ˌ(faɪv) ˌpɑːst ˈ.../
(five) to ... *phrase* /ˌ(faɪv) tə ˈ.../
a quarter past ... *phrase* /ə ˌkwɔːtə ˌpɑːst ˈ.../
a quarter to ... *phrase* /ə ˌkwɔːtə tə ˈ.../
half past ... *phrase* /ˌhɑːf ˌpɑːst ˈ.../
o'clock *phrase* /əˈklɒk/ **
birthday card *n* /ˈbɜːθdeɪ ˌkɑːd/
chat room *n* /ˈtʃæt ˌruːm/
country *n* /ˈkʌntri/ ***
email *n* /ˈiːmeɪl/ ***
food *n* /fuːd/ ***
letter *n* /ˈletə/ ***
listen *v* /ˈlɪsn/ ***
look *v* /lʊk/ ***
mobile phone *n* /ˌməʊbaɪl ˈfəʊn/ **
postcard *n* /ˈpəʊstˌkɑːd/ *
text message *n* /ˈtekst ˌmesɪdʒ/
write *v* /raɪt/ ***

Unit 4

first /fɜːst/ ***
second /ˈsekənd/ ***
third /θɜːd/
fourth /fɔːθ/
fifth /fɪfθ/
sixth /sɪksθ/
seventh /ˈsevnθ/
eighth /eɪtθ/
ninth /naɪnθ/
tenth /tenθ/
eleventh /ɪˈlevnθ/
twelfth /twelfθ/
thirteenth /ˌθɜːˈtiːnθ/
fourteenth /ˌfɔːˈtiːnθ/
fifteenth /ˌfɪfˈtiːnθ/
sixteenth /ˌsɪksˈtiːnθ/
seventeenth /ˌsevnˈtiːnθ/
eighteenth /ˌeɪˈtiːnθ/
nineteenth /ˌnaɪnˈtiːnθ/
twentieth /ˈtwentiəθ/
twenty-first /ˈtwenti ˌfɜːst/
thirtieth /ˈθɜːtiəθ/
thirty-first /ˈθɜːti ˌfɜːst/
January *n* /ˈdʒænjuəri/ ***
February *n* /ˈfebruəri/ ***
March *n* /mɑːtʃ/ ***
April *n* /ˈeɪprəl/ ***
May *n* /meɪ/ ***
June *n* /dʒuːn/ ***
July *n* /dʒʊˈlaɪ/ ***
August *n* /ˈɔːgəst/ ***
September *n* /sepˈtembə/ ***
October *n* /ɒkˈtəʊbə/ ***
November *n* /nəʊˈvembə/ ***
December *n* /dɪˈsembə/ ***
American *adj* /əˈmerɪkən/
Australia *n* /ɒˈstreɪliə/
Australian *adj* /ɒˈstreɪliən/
Brazil *n* /brəˈzɪl/
Britain *n* /ˈbrɪtn/
British *adj* /ˈbrɪtɪʃ/
Bulgaria *n* /bʌlˈgeəriə/
Chile *n* /ˈtʃɪli/
Columbia *n* /kəˈlʌmbiə/
France *n* /frɑːns/
French *adj* /frentʃ/
German *adj* /ˈdʒɜːmən/
Germany *n* /ˈdʒɜːməni/
India *n* /ˈɪndiə/
Indian *adj* /ˈɪndiən/
Italian *adj* /ɪˈtæliən/
Italy *n* /ˈɪtəli/
Japan *n* /dʒəˈpæn/
Japanese *adj* /ˌdʒæpənˈiːz/
Kenya *n* /ˈkenjə/
Kenyan *adj* /ˈkenjən/
Mexican *adj* /ˈmeksɪkən/
Mexico *n* /ˈmeksɪkəʊ/
Morocco *n* /məˈrɒkəʊ/
New Zealand *n* /ˌnjuː ˈziːlənd/
Poland *n* /ˈpəʊlənd/
Polish *adj* /ˈpəʊlɪʃ/
Romania *n* /ruˈmeɪniə/
Romanian *adj* /ruˈmeɪniən/
South Korea *n* /ˌsaʊθ kəˈrɪə/
Spain *n* /speɪn/
Spanish *adj* /ˈspænɪʃ/
Swiss *adj* /swɪs/
Switzerland *n* /ˈswɪtsələnd/
Taiwan *n* /taɪˈwæn/
Tanzania *n* /ˌtænzəˈnɪə/
the United States (of America) *n* /ðə juˌnaɪtɪd ˌsteɪts əv əˈmerɪkə/

Communication activities

Student A

Unit 3, Speaking Ex 1 page 11

Unit 3, Listening and speaking Ex 3 page 13

You're on holiday in (place) ________________, (country) ________________. It's (time) ________________, you're (activity) ________________. You phone your friend in (country) ________________ because you want to say what you are doing.

Unit 4, Vocabulary and speaking Ex 3 page 15

1 Read about some other international events. What kind of information is missing in each text? The place, the date or the kind of event?

Palio – Italy (________________________)
16th August

____

This very old Italian horse race takes place around the central square of the town of Siena in Tuscany.

Santa Claus World Championship – Switzerland (________________________)
26th November

This Swiss competition takes place at the end of November to start the winter. Over 100 Santas take part. There are prizes of €5,000.

International Mariachi Festival – Mexico (Guadalajara) 1st–11th September

This ________________________ takes place every year in September. There's music, dance, paintings, and lots of food and drink.

Winter Festival – India (Mount Abu)

____

When you're feeling hot in Rajasthan, go to Mount Abu. This Indian festival has music, dancing and watersports like boating on the lake.

International Film Festival – Poland (Warsaw)

____

There are over 130 films in cinemas across the Polish capital in this festival. They come from countries like Chile, Taiwan, and Bulgaria.

New Year Challenge – USA (New York City)
1st January

Start the New Year with ________________________ ________________ near Coney Island. Or perhaps keep your clothes on, stay warm, and watch.

2 Work with a partner. Ask your partner questions to find the missing information.
Example: *What kind of event is the … ? When does the … take place? Where does the … take place?*

Listening scripts

Unit 1 Worldwide

 Listening script 01

Reading text from page 3

 Listening script 02

(P = presenter, R = Rajab,
C = Cristina, H = Hisashi)

P: Today in 'This is home' I talk to foreigners who now live in Britain. Rajab Said and his wife Zainab are from Syria but live in York. Rajab, tell us a bit about York.

R: Well, we're happy here because we've got lots of good friends. I'm a student at the university, and there are lots of foreigners there. Not many Syrians though. York has got some good international food stores and restaurants, and there are some great shops – but it's an expensive city to live in.

P: Yes, but it's a very attractive city …

R: Yes, the city centre is old and very attractive. My favourite building is the Cathedral – York Minster. We go there with all our visitors from Syria. The countryside near York is very beautiful too, but the weather is terrible!

P: Cristina. You're from Spain but your home now is in Barrow. Is that right?

C: Yes, I live in Barrow-in-Furness. It's a large town in the north-west of England. I'm here for six months to practise my English. I like Barrow. It isn't very attractive and there are lots of factories, but there aren't many foreigners here – so I speak a lot of English.

Barrow hasn't got many historic sights, but the great thing about it is that it's by the sea and near the Lake District – a really beautiful area. The nightlife here is good too – and the people – the people are really friendly!

P: My third guest is from Japan. Hisashi, your home here is quite different, right?

H: That's right. I live in Eynsham - a small village near Oxford. I live with an English family. They've got three children and two dogs – and me, their foreign student. Eynsham is a beautiful village. It isn't very big and it's next to the River Thames. The village centre is old and very attractive and there are some small shops. There are seven pubs, but there isn't a cinema. It's very quiet here and very safe – but it isn't very interesting.

 Listening script 03

1 I'm a student at the university.
2 It's an expensive city to live in.
3 The countryside near York is beautiful.
4 It's a large town in the north-west of England.
5 I live with an English family.
6 It's next to the River Thames.
7 There isn't a cinema.

Unit 2 Other lives

 Listening script 04

Hello and welcome to Living Abroad – the programme about other people's lives.
We want to talk to you – our listeners around the world – about how you live and the things that matter to you.
What's great about your life?
Do you have any problems?
How do you spend your days?
I'd like you to meet our two guests, Sang Jin, and Annabel.

 Listening script 05

(S = Sang Jin, A = Annabel)

S: Hi. I'm Sang Jin. I come from Korea, but now I live in New Zealand. I'm a student here and my girlfriend is a New Zealander. Living here is very, very different from living in Korea. For example, I have a great relationship with my girlfriend's family and they really help me here. Most evenings I play the guitar and sing with my friend David at his apartment. I miss my family and friends in Korea, but I'm very happy here. My only problem is my girlfriend – yeah, my girlfriend! She doesn't like Korean food! Don't laugh. It's a big problem!

A: Hello. My name's Annabel Konkin. I live in Reykjavik, the capital of Iceland, but I don't come from Iceland. I'm a Californian. I'm a sports teacher and I work here as an aerobics instructor in a leisure centre.

Living in Iceland is really different from living in California. People get up early, go to bed early, and don't go out in the evenings in winter. This is all because of one thing – the weather. The weather here is something else! It's cold – but not really cold – and it's dark – dark all winter. Apart from the dark I have one other problem – the language. I don't speak or understand any Icelandic. That's OK in my classes. I give classes in English. But I don't understand street signs or anything on TV, and I have terrible problems sometimes with the telephone!

Listening script 06

1 comes
2 drinks
3 goes
4 has
5 kisses
6 lives
7 speaks
8 studies
9 watches
10 works

Listening script 07

Reading texts from page 8

Unit 3 It's a small world

 Listening script 08

1
(A = mother, B = teen boy)
A: 0258 0471
B: Hello, Mum?
A: Hi, Jon. Where are you?
B: At the station. Where's Dad? Is he working?
A: No, of course he isn't working. He's coming to pick you up. Don't worry. He'll be there soon.

2
(C = husband, D = wife)
C: Hi!
D: Hello. What are you doing?
C: Well, I'm still at the supermarket. I'm waiting to pay.
D: Could you get some beer? I forgot to put it on the list.
C: OK. How much?
D: A pack of 12 cans.
C: OK. Fine. Do we need anything else?
D: No, that's all, I think. See you soon.
C: Bye.

3
(E = woman, F = man)
E: Hello. Is that Terry Jones?
F: Speaking.
E: Listen. This is Emma Rose from Design Incorporated. I have a meeting with you this afternoon.
F: Yes, that's right. Everyone's waiting for you in the meeting room.
E: I'm really sorry. We're coming into Oxford on the M40 and the traffic is terrible. I'll be there in 10 minutes.
F: OK. Thank you for phoning. See you soon.
E: Yes. Thank you so much.

4
(G = teen boy, H = teen girl)
G: Hi, Julie. What do you want? What's that music? Are you watching MTV?
H: No, I'm not watching TV! I'm doing my maths homework. Have you got the answer to the last question?
G: Yes. It's easy.
H: What is it, then?
G: 99!
H: Right. Thanks. See you later then.

 Listening script 09

a thirty, thirteen
b fourteen, forty
c fifty, fifteen
d sixty, sixteen
e seventeen, seventy
f eighteen, eighty
g nineteen, ninety

Listening script 10

twenty one, eleven, twenty, fifty, one hundred, twenty three, seventeen, twenty-four, twenty-eight, eighty, thirteen, twenty-six, forty, fourteen, twenty-two, eighteen, twenty seven, twelve, sixty, fifteen, nineteen, seventy, ninety, twenty-nine, thirty, twenty-five, sixteen

Listening script 11

Reading text from page 12

Listening script 12

1 It's one o'clock.
2 It's ten past seven.
3 It's a quarter past four.
4 It's twenty-five past two.
5 It's half past six.
6 It's twenty to eight.
7 It's a quarter to nine.
8 It's ten to twelve.

Listening script 13

1
This is Radio Sydney, and the time is half past eleven. I am Charlie Snow and on the show today …

2
We will soon be landing in Istanbul. The local time is twenty-five past six and the weather on the ground is clear.

3
Here we are in Manchester at Old Trafford. It's five to three and kick off is in five minutes. It's a cold day here …

4
Hello and welcome to Breakfast with America. It's a beautiful day here in New York and it's a quarter past seven. So, if you're still in bed, it's time to get up and go for a run in the park.

5
The train now arriving at platform 2 is the 12 o'clock express from Cape Town to Johannesburg. Please stand clear of the line.

Listening script 14

(A = Amy, B = Brian)
A: 858 0373 Hello.
B: Hello. Can I speak to Amy please?
A: This is Amy. Who's that?
B: Hi, Amy. This is Brian.
A: Brian! Where are you?
B: I'm in New Zealand.
A: Wow! What time is it there?
B: It's half past seven in the morning.
A: And what are you doing?
B: Well, I'm having breakfast right now. How about you?
A: I'm making dinner.
B: Listen, Amy. Can you pick me up at the airport on Friday?
A: Yes, of course. What time?
B: The plane arrives at twenty past eight in the evening.
A: OK. No problem.
B: Thanks, Amy. That's very kind of you.
A: OK. See you on Friday then. Bye.
B: Bye!

Unit 4 This month

Listening script 15

Reading text from page 15

Listening script 16

1 My birthday's on 4th April.
2 My girlfriend's birthday is on 19th March.
3 Our wedding anniversary's on 13th June.
4 I'm getting married on 28th October.
5 We start school again on 31st January.
6 My holiday starts on 15th July.
7 I've got a driving test on 27th November.
8 My new job starts on 31st May.

Listening script 17

Country and nationality words from Ex 1 page 16

Listening script 18

(I= Interviewer, W = Wendy Bowler, K = Krishnan Tate)
I: Hi, Wendy. Is this your first race?
W: No, it isn't. It's my third.
I: What's your target time?
W: Well, I usually take about five hours, but I'm not feeling very well today, so I don't know …
I: Can you tell me about your clothes? You're wearing a banana costume!
W: Yes. When I run, I always wear something crazy. It's more fun for the spectators – and for the other runners.
I: How often do you train for the marathon?
W: I run every morning and I sometimes run in the evenings too, if the weather is OK. My boyfriend is running today too, and we often go running together at weekends. It's our hobby.
I: The race starts in 15 minutes. How are you feeling now?
W: Terrible. I want to go home and go to bed. I'm always nervous before the race!

I: We're here in Greenwich near the river with Krishnan Tate. Krishnan, do you always watch the race from here?
K: No. This is my first time. I usually watch it on television. The traffic is always terrible on marathon day.
I: Why are you here today then?
K: Well, some of my friends from college are running and I want to see them.
I: Why aren't you running with them?
K: Me? I never go running. I hate it!
I: And what do you think of the marathon?
K: It's great! I'm really having fun. It's like a big street party! I hardly ever come to London, but this is great. So I think I'll come and see the marathon every year from now on!

Unit 5 Review

Listening script 19

(A = man, B = woman)
1
A: I'm hungry. Do you want to go for a meal?
B: Yes, OK. Are there any good restaurants near here?
A: There are lots. What kind of food do you like? Indian, Chinese, Mexican?
B: How about Indian? I love Indian food but we hardly ever eat it at home.
A: OK. I know a good place. Shall we go now?
B: Is it far?
A: No, it isn't. It's just round the corner.
B: Great. Let's go.

(C = woman, D = man)
2
C: Hi! How are you?
D: Hi! It's nice to see you. What are you doing here?
C: I'm looking for a present for my brother. It's his birthday on 5th May.
D: What kind of music does he like?
C: Well, he loves guitar music and he plays the guitar. The problem is I never listen to guitar music.
D: Does he like Spanish music?
C: Yes, he does.
D: Let's see. Has he got this CD? It's great.
C: Let me see. No, he hasn't. That's a good idea. Thanks for your help.

Listening script 20

Song from page 20

Communication activities

Student B

Unit 3, Speaking Ex 1 page 11

Unit 3, Listening and speaking Ex 3, page 13

It's (time) ________________. You're asleep in bed. It's very cold in your house and you aren't feeling very well. How do you feel when (friend) ________________ phones? ________________

Unit 4, Vocabulary and speaking Ex 3 page 15

1 Read about some other international events. What kind of information is missing in each text? The place, the date or the kind of event?

Palio – Italy (Siena) 16th August

This very old ____________________________ takes place around the central square of the town of Siena in Tuscany.

International Mariachi Festival – Mexico (Guadalajara)

____________________________________.

This Mexican music festival takes place every year in September. There's music, dance, paintings, and lots of food and drink.

International Film Festival – Poland (____________________________)

13th–22nd October

There are over 130 films in cinemas across the Polish capital in this festival. They come from countries like Chile, Taiwan, and Bulgaria.

Santa Claus World Championship – Switzerland (Samnaun)

____

This Swiss competition takes place in Samnaun to start the winter. Over 100 Santas take part. There are prizes of €5,000.

Winter Festival – India (Mount Abu)

29th–31st December

When you're feeling hot in Rajasthan, go to Mount Abu. This Indian festival has ________________ ______________ and ________________ ______________ like boating on the lake.

New Year Challenge – USA (________________ ________________) 1st January

Start the New Year with a swim in the icy cold sea near Coney Island. Or perhaps keep your clothes on, stay warm, and watch.

2 Work with a partner. Ask your partner questions to find the missing information.

Example: *What kind of event is the .... ? When does the .... take place? Where does the ... take place?*

Module 2
Ourselves

1 Being different

LEARNING AIMS

- Can talk about abilities
- Can describe clothes
- Can choose and buy clothes

Lead-in

1 Which of these statements do you agree with? Discuss your ideas.

- Your first impressions of people are very important.
- It's difficult to be happy if you don't have a perfect body.
- Plastic surgery is a great idea if you want to change your body.
- It's important to be happy with yourself as you are.
- Your clothes say a lot about who you are.

Short and tall

Reading

1 Look at the photos with the articles. Who do you think has these problems? Write *S* (Sandy), *J* (Jackie) or *B* (both) in the boxes.

1 It's difficult to drive a car. ☐

2 People in public places look at you all the time. ☐

3 It's difficult to use a lift. ☐

4 It's difficult to hear people when they talk to you. ☐

5 It's uncomfortable to use public transport. ☐

6 It's difficult to buy clothes. ☐

2 21 Read the articles quickly. Which of the problems in Ex 1 do they mention?

3 Read the texts again and answer the questions.

1 Why do people look at Sandy and her husband?
2 Why does Sandy need a good imagination?
3 How does Sandy feel about being short?
4 What is the Europatreffen?
5 How do very tall people feel about public transport and public places?
6 Why is Jim Briggs happy with his height?

4 Work with a partner. What is the secret of happiness? Discuss your ideas.

Sandy Marshall

I am 4ft 2in*

People remember me and my husband. When we go to the supermarket together I see people thinking, 'There are two of them!' My husband Andrew is small too. He's 4ft 6in*.The world is not made for someone like me. You need imagination to solve the problems. When I go to people's houses I can't reach the doorbells. In lifts I go up to the floor I can reach and then I get out and walk up the stairs. People often ask me, 'Can you imagine your life as a tall person?' I say, 'I can't. This is me.' I can't imagine anything different. I'm not saying it's easy being so short. It isn't, but it's about learning to live with your body. I'm happy with myself. And I feel special. Being short is my life.

*in = inch (1 in = 2.5 cm)

I am 4ft 2in by Sandy Marshall as told to Paula Cocozza for *The Guardian Weekend*

Invasion of the tall PEOPLE

This week the *Europatreffen* – a meeting for tall people from around the world – is taking place in Edinburgh. Jackie Timbs, a member of the Tall Persons Club (TPC) for Great Britain and Ireland is one of the organisers. 'Here I can look at people when I talk to them,' says Jackie. 'It's so nice. I usually bend down because I can't hear properly. This week I can stand up straight. 'Most cities in Britain are difficult for tall people. We can't sit comfortably on trains and buses,' says Timbs. 'We can't eat or sleep comfortably either, because restaurant tables are usually too low and hotel beds aren't long enough. Buying clothes is a big problem too.' Jim Briggs, 6ft 9in*, is a member of the London TPC. 'Many people have problems with their height when they first come to club meetings,' he says, 'But people in the club are very friendly and positive. Thanks to the club, I am happy with my height now, and I actually enjoy being tall.'

*4ft 2in = 1 metre 27 cm
*4ft 6in = 1 metre 37 cm
*6ft 9in = 2 metres 5 cm

LANGUAGE STUDY

Talking about ability: *can / can't*

1 Complete these sentences about the picture with *can* and *can't*.

1 *Pete* ____________ *reach the doorbell.*
2 *Alice* ____________ *reach the doorbell.*

2 What form of the verb do we use after *can / can't*?

Grammar reference page 58

Pronunciation ***can / can't***

1 **22** Listen and repeat the different ways we say *can* and *can't*.

1 can /kən/ I can sleep on buses or trains – no problem!
2 can't /kɑːnt/ I can't sleep after a big meal.
3 can /kæn/ I can.

2 Choose the correct alternative to complete the pronunciation rules.

1 We say the *weak/strong* form of *can* in short answers and at the end of sentences.
2 We usually say the *weak/strong* form of *can* in questions and in the middle of a sentence.
3 There is only one way of saying *can/can't*. It has no weak form.

Listening and speaking

1 23 Listen to Matt. Tick (✓) the things he can do. Cross (✗) the things he can't do.

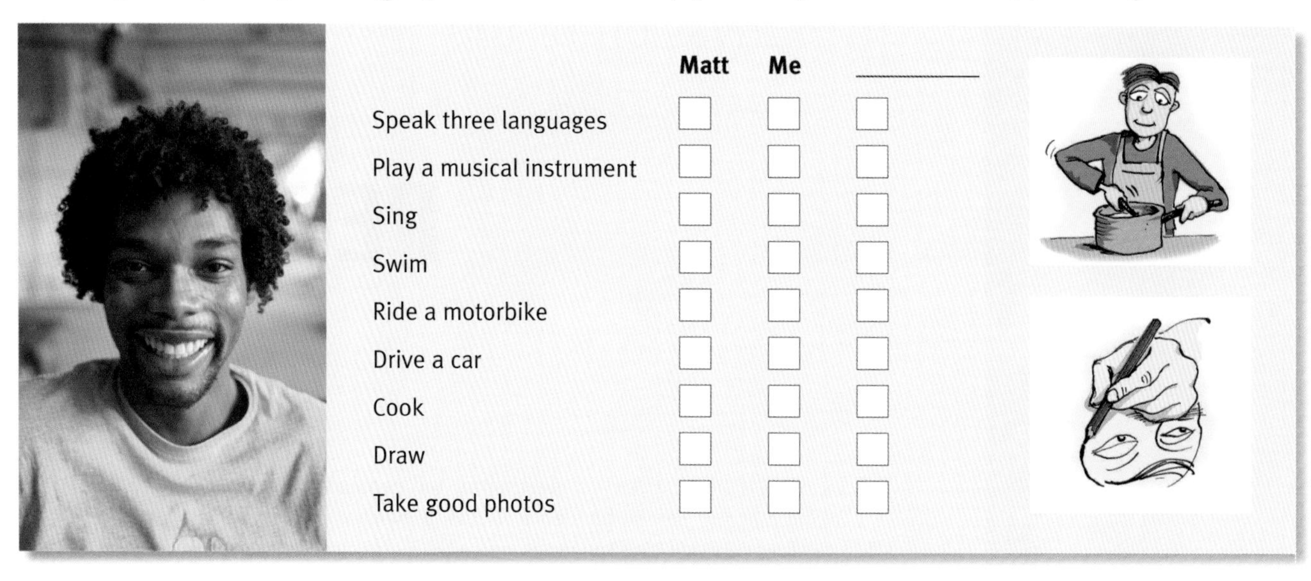

	Matt	Me	______
Speak three languages			
Play a musical instrument			
Sing			
Swim			
Ride a motorbike			
Drive a car			
Cook			
Draw			
Take good photos			

2 Complete the list for yourself and then for your partner.

Example: A: *Can you play a musical instrument?*
B: *Yes, I can. / No, I can't, but I'd like to learn the piano.*

3 Tell the class one thing that is different about you and your partner.

Example: *Paula can ride a motorbike, but I can't.*

A question of style

Vocabulary and speaking

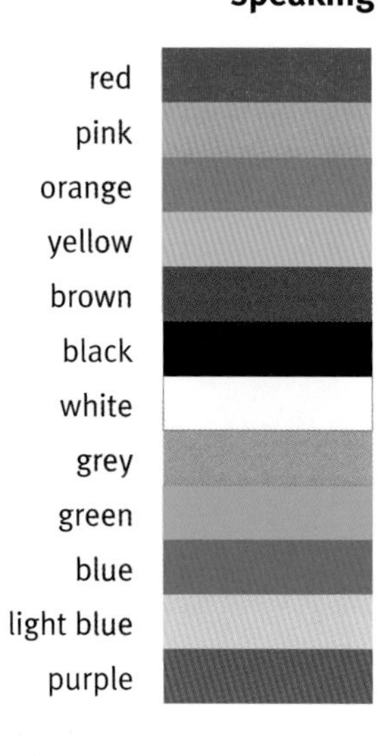

1 Read the descriptions and complete the labels with the words in **bold**.

1 Alex is wearing a smart **jacket** and **trousers**. He's got a pink **shirt** with a red **tie** and a black **coat**. His **shoes** are black.

2 Grace is wearing a purple **skirt**, a brown **belt** and a white **top**. She is also wearing a yellow **scarf**, a pink hat and brown **boots**.

3 Sarah is looking casual in blue **jeans**, white **trainers**, orange **T-shirt** and a green **jumper**. She's also wearing a red scarf and a grey **hat**.

2 Do you like the clothes in the pictures? Talk about them like this.

A: *I like Grace's boots.*
B: *I don't like her skirt very much.*

3 Write sentences about your style in clothes.

Example:
I wear dark-coloured tops most of the time. Hats don't suit me. I've got a lot of different jumpers.

4 Give your sentences to your teacher. Your teacher will give you someone else's sentences. Ask your classmates questions and find the correct person.

Example: *What do you wear most of the time?*

Listening and speaking

1 **24** Listen to a dialogue in a clothes shop. What does the customer buy?

2 Read the dialogue and complete the gaps with the phrases in the box.

Have you got a size 14? Can I help you? Can I pay by credit card? Can I try them on? How much is that? I'm looking for I'll take it

A: Good morning. ____________________
B: Yes, please. ____________________ something to wear to a wedding.
A: How about a skirt and top?
B: Oh, yes. I love these. ____________________.
A: Of course. The changing room's over there …
B: Excuse me. The skirt's a bit small. ____________________
A: Yes, here you are.
B: That's perfect. ____________________ and the top too. And have you got any earrings?
A: Yes, we have. Here you are.
B: Those are pretty. I'll have them too. ____________________
A: £131.49 please.
B: ____________________
A: Yes, of course.

NOTE

See page 64 for a size conversion chart.

3 Listen again and check your answers.

4 Work with a partner. Student A you are shopping for clothes. Turn to page 61. Student B you are a shop assistant. Turn to page 64. Act out a dialogue using the phrases in Ex 2.

CD-ROM For more activities go to **Ourselves Unit 1**

2 Family matters

LEARNING AIMS

- Can express likes and dislikes
- Can talk about families
- Can talk about free time activities

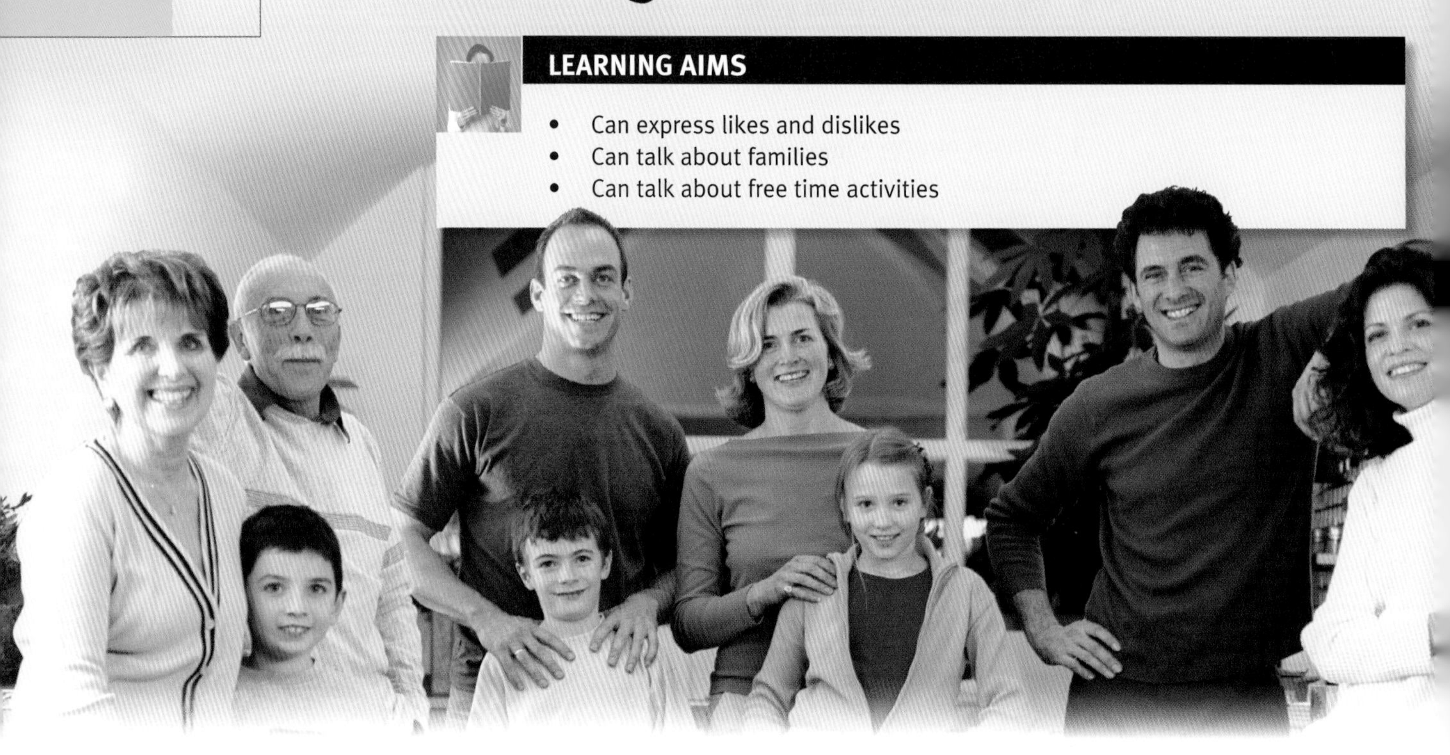

Lead-in

1 Look at the photo. How old do you think the people are?

		early	teens	forties	
in	his	mid	twenties	fifties	seventies
	her	late	thirties	sixties	eighties

2 What do people usually do at different stages of their lives in your country? Discuss, using these ideas and adding ideas of your own.

buy a house   buy a sports car   fall in love for the first time   get married
get their first job   go to university   have children / grandchildren
learn to drive   open a bank account   put on weight   retire   take exams

Example: *In my country, people usually retire in their mid sixties.*

Relatives

Vocabulary and listening

1 Look at the family tree. Ask and answer questions about Adam's family using these words.

aunt   brother   cousin   daughter   father   grandchildren   grandparent
mother   nephew   niece   parents   sister   son   uncle

Example: **A:** *Who are Jasmin and Ian?* **B:** *Jasmin is Adam's aunt and Ian's his uncle.*

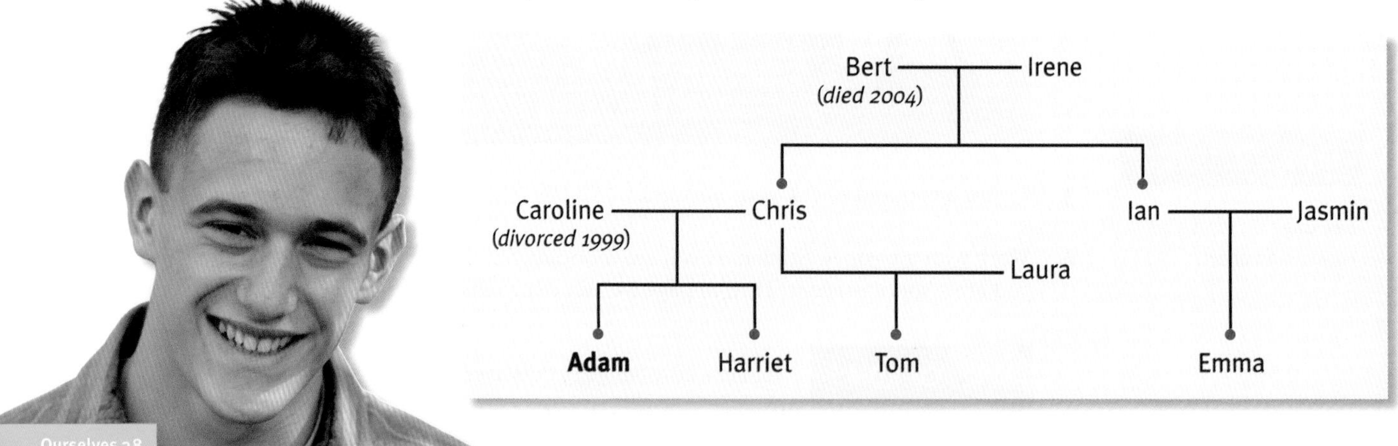

2 25 Listen to Adam. Are these statements true (T) or false (F)?

1 Adam's got a part-time job.
2 His father is married to an Italian woman.
3 His sister is a student at university.
4 Adam and his cousin see each other often.
5 His grandmother is retired.

3 Draw your family tree. Tell a partner about your relatives.
Example: *My cousin David is at university. He's got a girlfriend but they don't live together.*

LANGUAGE STUDY

Expressing likes and dislikes

1 Look at these sentences from the listening in Ex 2. Which sentences have positive meanings, which have negative meanings and which have neutral meanings?

I can't stand *shopping.* *She* ***loves*** *being in Africa.* *I* ***don't mind*** *staying there in the summer.* *She* ***doesn't like*** *doing any sports.*

2 Look at the sentences in Ex 1 and Listening script 25 on page 62. Find all the sentences that express likes, dislikes and preferences and write them in three lists.

Positive meanings (✓)	Negative meanings (✗)	Neutral meanings (✓✗)
	I can't stand shopping.	

3 Look at the sentences in your lists and complete the correct alternative.
We follow phrases about likes and dislikes with ___.

a the infinitive b the *-ing* form of the verb

Grammar reference page 58

4 Complete these sentences about Adam and his family with the correct form of the verbs in the box.

be buy fly go live look after speak stay study

1 Laura likes ____________ in England but she misses Spain.
2 Adam prefers ____________ in London with his dad.
3 Irene doesn't like ____________ retired.
4 Adam enjoys ____________ at university.
5 Harriet hates ____________ to people when she doesn't know them.
6 Harriet doesn't mind ____________ her half brother.
7 Emma loves ____________ shopping and ____________ new clothes.
8 Caroline can't stand ____________, so she never travels anywhere.

5 Work with a partner. Talk about you and your family. Use the table to help you.

go on holiday spend New Year's Eve go out have Sunday lunch speak on the phone go shopping for clothes	with	my parents my children my friends my sisters / brothers my grandparents my girlfriend / boyfriend

Examples:
I don't mind going on holiday with my parents.
I can't stand shopping for clothes with my grandmother.

We like different things

Reading **1** Look at the photo of Tim and his son Jasper. Who do you think each sentence is about? Write *T* (Tim) or *J* (Jasper).

He likes:

1 sitting in the garden. ☐
2 listening to rock music. ☐
3 going out with friends. ☐
4 driving fast. ☐
5 watching art films. ☐
6 going to the theatre. ☐
7 watching Hollywood blockbusters on DVD. ☐
8 sending text messages. ☐

2 **26** Work with a partner. Student A read Tim's account of the day he shared with Jasper. Student B read Jasper's account. Check your answers in Ex 1. Does anything surprise you?

Generation gap

Tim Collins and his son Jasper share each others' favourite activities for a day

Tim

My son and I like different kinds of music. My idea of a perfect evening is playing air guitar* while listening to rock – usually *Status Quo*, the *Rolling Stones* or *The Who*. Jasper shuts himself in his bedroom and listens to opera. He loves it, but for me it's just an awful noise! Most evenings Jasper and I argue about noise. He says that I have the TV on too loud – like an old person. What a cheek! He only enjoys listening to his music if it's very, very loud!

Today I sit on Jasper's bed and we listen to Mozart's *The Marriage of Figaro* together – his choice! I don't understand the Italian words. I'm exhausted when I leave his room.

Jasper and I are very different. He's more similar to his mother. He's a very sociable person. He texts his friends about every 15 minutes, and he goes out with them about three or four times a week. I prefer staying at home. I enjoy sitting in the garden or reading a book. Every weekend I watch a Hollywood blockbuster on DVD. One of the only things we have in common is our passion for cars. Jasper loves driving fast and so do I! Next time we have a day together I want to go rally driving with him. We're both competitive and like winning – so that should be fun.

Jasper

I don't mind going to the theatre with Dad. I go and see an opera once or twice a year. But watching plays is a bit boring. I love going to the cinema, but Dad and I don't like the same films. I prefer going with my mum or my friends. We don't go often – less than once a month, I guess. But we enjoy watching art films and having a good time together.

When Dad chooses to go to the theatre with me, I agree, but only after he agrees to listen to some of my music. He spends every evening listening to old rock songs. I can't stand them. I turn up my opera music really loud so I can't hear them!

The play we see – *Rock 'n' Roll* – is all about politics in Prague in the 1960s and 1980s. It's OK. It makes me think about how politics can change people's lives. Dad loves the play. He says it's brilliant. I don't mind it, but I'm not really into watching plays.

Dad can't stand opera – and I choose *The Marriage of Figaro* for him to listen to. It's really funny watching his face while he sits on my bed and listens to Mozart's music. I know he hates it! Next time we spend a day together I want to go for a drive. Dad's car is really fast and we both enjoy driving.

Glossary *playing air guitar = playing an imaginary guitar

3 Read your text again. Answer your questions.

Student A

1 What does Tim like doing in the evening?
2 What does Tim think of Jasper's music?
3 What does Tim do with Jasper?
4 What kind of films does Tim enjoy?
5 What do they both enjoy doing?

Student B

1 What does Tim choose to do with Jasper?
2 What kind of films does Jasper enjoy?
3 What kind of music does Jasper listen to?
4 What do they think of the play?
5 What do they both enjoy doing?

4 Work with a partner. Explain the answers to your questions in Ex 3.

5 What do you have in common with Tim or with Jasper? Discuss your ideas.

Vocabulary and speaking

1 Put these frequency phrases in order, from very frequent (1) to hardly ever (4).

once or twice a year ☐ less than once a month ☐

three or four times a week ☐ most evenings ☐

2 Find three more frequency phrases in the reading texts. Then ask and answer these questions with a partner.

How often do you …

- listen to really loud music?
- spend a day with your mother / father?
- watch a Hollywood blockbuster?
- go for a long drive?

3 Work with a partner. Find out how your partner feels about these activities and when they do them.

dancing going to pop concerts going for walks going to the gym going to the theatre/cinema jogging listening to music playing video games having a drink with friends watching TV or DVDs

Example:

A: *Do you like watching DVDs?*
B: *Yes, I do. I love it.*

A: *What kind of films do you like?*
B: *A mixture – horror, comedy, love stories.*

A: *How often do you go to the cinema?*
B: *About twice a month. How about you?*

CD-ROM For more activities go to **Ourselves Unit 2**

3 Are you crazy?

LEARNING AIMS

- Can use countable and uncountable nouns
- Can describe where things are
- Can talk about routines

Extreme collecting

Lead-in

1 Do you collect anything? Where do you keep your collection? Do you know anyone with an unusual collection? Tell the class.

Reading and vocabulary

1 **27** Read the article about collections on page 43 and complete the table.

	Mandisa	Carlos	Jeff	Angie
What?				
How many?				
Where?				

2 What do you remember? Complete the names.

1 __________’s collection takes up a lot of room.
2 __________ keeps her collection all over her room.
3 __________ wants to give the collection to a museum.
4 __________ spends all his free time collecting.
5 __________’s collection is worth a lot of money.
6 __________ has more than 2,000 items from all over the world.
7 __________’s collection is under the house.

3 Read the text again and check your answers.

4 Imagine you are a museum manager. You can keep one of the collections. Which one would you choose? Why? Discuss your ideas with a partner.

Example:
A: *I’d keep the marble collection because children love looking at beautiful things.*
B: *Really? I’d choose … / I wouldn’t choose … because …*

5 Look at the pictures on page 43 and match the two halves of the sentences.

1	The marbles are	a	in front of Jeff.
2	There’s a red sign	b	on the bananas.
3	The drum is	c	under a large one.
4	There are some labels	d	next to the mandolin.
5	There’s a small instrument	e	behind Jeff.
6	There are some beer cans	f	in a box.

6 Think of three things that belong to you – one old, one interesting and one valuable. Work with a partner. Explain where your things are.

Example:
I’ve got an interesting African mask. It’s on the wall next to the windows in my bedroom.

CRAZY Collections

Be careful! Collecting can take over your life!

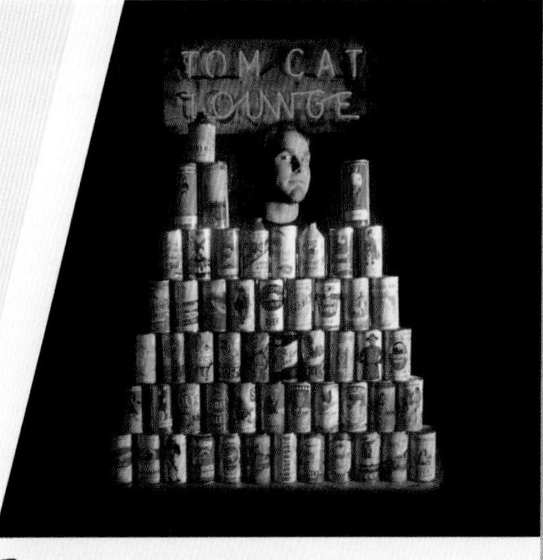

Source: *Beer Can Man* by Monster Maysh for *Loaded magazine*

Music mania

Carlos Blanco collects musical instruments. Four hundred of his instruments are in a museum, and he keeps the rest of his collection of more than 2,000 instruments in a large room in his house near Alicante, Spain. Carlos, a musician, travels all over the world collecting the instruments, and he can play all of them. 'I love my house in Alicante,' says Carlos, 'but I love travelling too – and my collection is my obsession now. I spend all my free time on my instruments!'

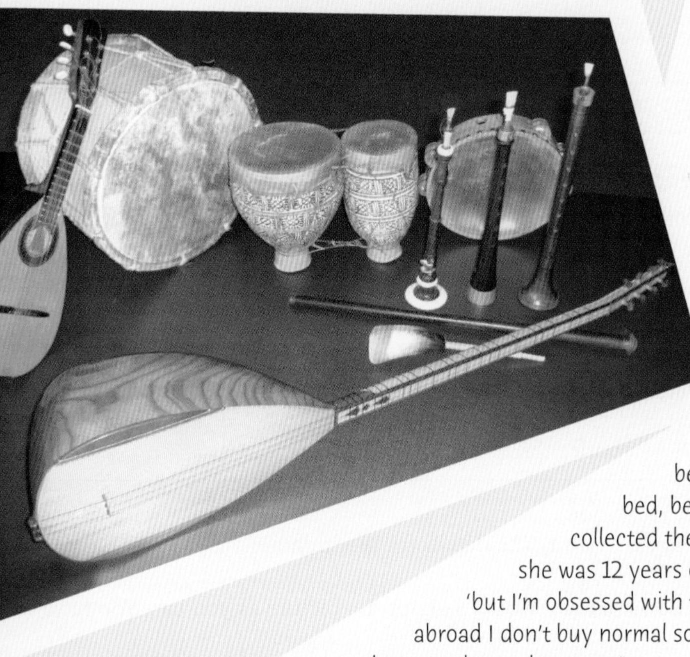

Beer can man

Jeff Lebo is a beer can collector. His teenage hobby is now his obsession, and his collection is worth £160,000. 'It's insane,*' says Jeff. He keeps his collection in a special building next to his house, and the building is bigger than his house! Jeff has got 55,000 cans but he is still collecting. 'I love British cans,' he tells us. But there are still lots that he hasn't got. 'Finding them gets me up in the morning,' he adds. By the way, there isn't any beer in the cans. Jeff buys them empty because he doesn't drink beer!

Glossary * insane = crazy

She's bananas!

Angie Knox's collection doesn't take up a lot of space. In fact, she keeps her collection of more than 400 banana labels in her bedroom. 'I stick them on my wardrobe doors, on my bed, behind the door – anywhere that there's room!' Angie collected the first label from her favourite fruit when she was 12 years old. 'I love bananas,' she says, 'but I'm obsessed with the labels. When I go abroad I don't buy normal souvenirs, I buy – and eat – bananas.'

It's marbellous!

Mandisa Sakara's marbles are under the ground. Mandisa's house in Cape Town, South Africa, has a large room under the house where she keeps her collection of more than a million marbles. 'I haven't got any special furniture or equipment for them,' she says. 'I just keep them all in boxes.' Mandisa doesn't want to sell her collection. She wants to give it to the local Toy Museum. 'It's my passion, and I want to share it with others.'

LANGUAGE STUDY

Countable and uncountable nouns

1 Look at the two groups of nouns. Which group has words we can count (countable nouns)? Which group has words we can't count (uncountable nouns)?

Group A: water, time, music, beer, space, money, furniture
Group B: marble, room, banana, can, musical instrument, dollar, wardrobe

2 Underline the nouns in these sentences and complete the table.

1 *There's a large room underground.*
2 *There are some valuable instruments.*
3 *Have you got any beer?*
4 *There's an interesting Arabic instrument.*
5 *There aren't any Russian labels.*
6 *There's some special furniture.*

Nouns	*a / an*	*some / any*
Singular, countable		
Plural, countable		
Uncountable		

3 Look at the sentences with *some* and *any* in Ex 2 again and choose the correct alternative.

1 We use *some / any* in positive sentences.
2 We use *some / any* in negative sentences.
3 We usually use *some / any* in questions.

Grammar reference pages 58–59

4 Complete the text with *a / an, some* or *any*.

Home Search Shop Bookmarks

JAMIE PROUT of London, collects *Star Wars* souvenirs. He has (1) ____ enormous collection of 20,000 *Star Wars* items. His favourites in his collection are (2) ____ original Darth Vader costume and (3) ____ C3PO robot. 'I keep my collection in (4) ____ large room in the attic. I never have (5) ____ money because I spend it on my collection.' Jamie has got (6) ____ *Star Wars* books in Chinese and (7) ____ *Star Wars* dolls from Russia. 'In Korea they make a lot of *Star Wars* figures,' he says. 'I haven't got (8) ____ Korean figures, but I want to buy some.'

5 Turn to the picture on page 61. Study the details for one minute.

6 Work with a partner. Write as many sentences about the picture as you can. You have five minutes.

Example:
There are two guitars on the wall. There's some 90s bedroom furniture on the left.

7 Check your sentences with the class. Which pair wrote the most correct sentences?

In my collection ...

8 You have a collection of special items. Think of three unusual things you have in your collection.

Example:
Some sea shells, some used phone cards, some baseball caps ...

9 Work in groups. Play the game. Start like this:

A: *In my collection I've got some sea shells.*
B: *In my collection I've got some sea shells and some used international phone cards.*
C: *In my collection ...*

Little things

Reading and vocabulary

1 28 Do you have any strange habits? Complete the quiz to find out.

ARE YOU OBSESSIVE? Do our quiz to find out

1 **There are some dirty plates in the kitchen. What do you do?**

- a Sit down and watch TV. I can wash them up tomorrow.
- b Wash them up. I can't relax when there's something dirty in the house.
- c Start watching TV, but feel bad about not washing them up.

2 **You're driving to the airport to go on holiday. You don't remember turning off your home computer. What do you do?**

- a Phone a neighbour and ask, 'Can you check my computer?'
- b Drive back home and check the computer.
- c Forget it. You can turn it off when you come back.

3 **How tidy is your home?**

- a When something's on the floor, I pick it up, so the house is quite tidy.
- b Everything in my house is always in perfect order.
- c It isn't. I have more important things to do.

4 **What do you do with your old clothes?**

- a I can't stand clutter. When I don't wear things for a time, I throw them away.
- b I never throw anything away.
- c Once a year I throw things away.

If you've got two or more b answers, you are a little obsessive. Take things easy and enjoy life!

2 Find these phrases in the quiz. What do the words in **bold** refer to?

Wash **them** up. You can turn **it** off. I pick **it** up. I throw **them** away.

3 Match the phrases in column A to the phrases in column B.

A		B	
1	The lights are on.	a	Pick them up.
2	Your CDs are all over the floor.	b	Turn them off.
3	Let's watch TV.	c	Put it down.
4	This suitcase is heavy.	d	Put them on.
5	Those are nice earrings.	e	Turn it on.

4 29 Listen and check your answers.

5 Work with a partner. Choose one of the exchanges in Ex 3 and prepare a similar dialogue. Perform your dialogue for the class. As you listen to other students, tick (✓) the phrases in Ex 3 that you hear.

Listening and speaking

1 30 Listen to a part of a radio programme about strange routines. Number these situations in the order you hear about them.

- a going on a journey ☐
- b going out in the morning ☐
- c doing an exam ☐
- d going to bed ☐
- e preparing for something important ☐

2 What do the people do in the different situations? Listen again and make notes.

3 Which of the routines do you think are normal? Which do you find really strange?

4 Work with a partner. Discuss your special routines. Think about what you do before …

- you go to bed
- you leave the house
- an important occasion
- an exam
- a long journey

CD-ROM For more activities go to **Ourselves Unit 3**

4 Men and women

LEARNING AIMS

- Can talk about the past
- Can talk about chores and who does them
- Can write short texts about people's lives

It's a chore

Lead-in

1 Match the chores to the objects in the pictures.

do the cleaning	☐	do the cooking	☐	do the gardening	☐
do the ironing	☐	do the shopping	☐	do the washing	☐
do the washing up	☐	make the beds	☐	sweep the floor	☐
take out the rubbish	☐				

1 2 3 4 5 6 7 8 9 10

2 Who does each of these chores in your home? Discuss with a partner.

Reading

1 31 Read the blog extracts on page 47 quickly and complete the best title.

- Home life
- Mum's strike
- What a week!

2 Read the text again and answer these questions.

1. What's Debbie's job?
2. Why did she start her strike?
3. Who made dinner on the first day of Debbie's strike?
4. Why did Chris and Mike go shopping?
5. Who did the chores while Debbie was on strike?
6. How long did her strike last?

3 Discuss these questions.

1. Do you think Debbie was a fool to allow her children to eat all the pizza? Why?
2. What do you think of her husband, Mike?
3. Did Debbie need to go on strike? Why?
4. What's the right age for children to learn to do chores?

4 Which of these statements do you agree with? Why?

1. It's a good idea for men and women to share household tasks equally.
2. Men are good at some chores and women are good at others.
3. Men usually work long hours, so they need more time to rest at home than women.
4. Most women like doing housework.
5. Men can't do more than one thing at a time.

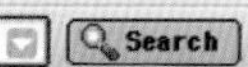

I'm not sure when it started. Perhaps it was when my 14-year-old daughter Claire looked in the fridge and asked, 'Why isn't there anything nice to eat?' Or maybe it was when my husband said, 'I'd like you to iron my shirt today. I've got an important meeting tomorrow'. But at that moment I thought: '*That's enough!*' My husband, Mike, is an accountant. I work from home. I'm an editor. I never do just one thing. I wash up while I print out texts. I do the washing while I write emails, and so on. And the problem? My husband and three children don't see what I do at home, and they don't do anything to help!

THURSDAY, DAY 1

On the first day of my strike I did the cleaning in the morning. Then I stopped doing chores and started my strike. I worked in my office all afternoon.
In the evening Sam (seven years old) left all his toys on the floor. 'Mum's on strike,' I said. And he picked them all up! Mike and my two older children made toast for dinner. I made myself pizza.
I'm stupid. The kids were hungry and ate it all – and I had nothing!

SATURDAY, DAY 3

Chris (16 years old) came into the kitchen at breakfast time. He opened the fridge and looked in. 'Where's all the food?' he asked. 'You didn't do the shopping,' I said. Later that day he went to the shops with his dad.

MONDAY, DAY 5

I'm feeling happy. Mike cooked dinner last night. Chris washed up and cleaned his bedroom and Claire did the washing and the ironing.
'Well done,' I said.
'It's not difficult, Mum,' Chris answered.

WEDNESDAY, DAY 7

Today I ended my strike. In the evening we all watched a video together.
'Is your strike over, Mum?' Sam asked.
'Maybe. Did you learn anything this week?'
'Yes, I did. I can make my bed now.'
'That's good,' I said. 'Your older brother didn't learn to do that for a very long time!'

LANGUAGE STUDY

Talking about the past

The past simple

1 Look at these sentences. Underline the verbs and answer the questions.

a *I cook dinner while I write emails.* b *I worked in my office all afternoon.*

1 Which sentence is about things that happen all the time? 2 Which sentence is about the past?

2 Underline the past simple verbs in the article. Use the verbs you have underlined to complete the lists with the past forms of the verbs.

Regular verbs

start ____________
look ____________
ask ____________
stop ____________
work ____________
drop ____________
pick up ____________
open ____________
clean ____________
answer ____________
end ____________
watch ____________

Irregular verbs

be (I, he, she, it) ____________
say ____________
think ____________
have ____________
do ____________
make ____________
be (you, we, they) ____________
eat ____________
go ____________

NOTE

In regular verbs ending in short vowel + consonant, the last consonant is doubled.

drop → dropped
stop → stopped

3 How do we form the past simple form of regular verbs?

4 32 Listen to the past forms of the regular verbs in the table below. How do we pronounce the *-ed* ending? Tick (✓) the sound you hear for each verb.

	/t/	/d/	/ɪd/
1 look			
2 start			
3 answer			
4 stop			
5 open			
6 end			

5 Complete these sentences from the text and answer the questions.

Question: *'______ you ______ anything this week?'*
Negative: *'Your older brother ______ ______ to do that for a long time!'*

1 Which two verbs are in both the sentences?
2 Which verb uses the past tense form?
3 Which verb uses the infinitive form?

6 Complete the rule with the words *do* and the main verb.

To make questions or negative sentences in the past simple we use the past simple of ______ and the infinitive of ______.

Grammar reference page 59

7 Complete the text using the past simple.

New Message

Today, when I (1 go) ____________ down for breakfast, there (2 be) ____________ no milk. I (3 eat) ____________ my cereal without milk. Silvie (4 have) ____________ a coffee. Matt (5 come) ____________ into the kitchen. He (6 look) ____________ confused and he (7 not say) ____________ anything. I (8 say) ____________ goodbye and (9 go) ____________ to my class. This evening Silvie (10 make) ____________ dinner and Matt (11 clean) ____________ the sitting room – but he (12 not do) ____________ the washing up!

8 Complete the sentences to make questions about yesterday.

1 What / you / have / for breakfast?
2 you / buy / anything?
3 How / you / go / to your class?
4 How many / hours / you / sleep?
5 Which household chores / you / do?
6 What / you / do / in the evening?

9 33 Listen and repeat the questions.

10 Ask other students the questions in Ex 8. Tell the class one interesting thing you learnt.
Example: *Karl came to class by car. But it wasn't in his car. It was in his brother's car.*

Gender challenge

Listening and vocabulary

1 Do men or women usually do these jobs in your country? Why?

2 34 Listen to Darren. Which of the jobs does he do?

3 Listen again and match the two columns to make sentences about Darren.

1 Darren was born
2 His father was
3 He started dancing
4 His older sister
5 He went to ballet school

a when he was eight.
b a builder.
c in London.
d in Manchester.
e went to ballet classes.

4 35 Listen to Carlita. Complete the factfile notes about her.

factfile

Name: ***Carlita Daniel***
Occupation: ____________________
Place of birth: ____________________
Year of birth: ____________________
Family: ____________________
Age started racing go-karts: ____________________
Age started racing cars: ____________________
Lives: ____________________

Writing

1 Choose one of these options:

1 Use your notes about Carlita to write a short biography of her life. Start like this: *Carlita Daniel is a racing driver. She was born …*

2 Write a short biography about someone you know well, for example, a friend or a relative. Prepare factfile notes before you start.

CD-ROM For more activities go to **Ourselves Unit 4**

5 Review

Lead-in

1 Write names on small pieces of paper of a person you …

- really enjoy being with.
- phone if you have a problem.
- were very close to but don't see much now.
- disagree with sometimes.

2 Work with a partner. Swap pieces of paper. Ask questions to find out who the people are and what their relationship is with your partner.

Example:
A: *Is Danny your boyfriend?*
B: *No, he isn't. He's an old friend.*
A: *How did you meet him?*
B: *I met him outside my house. We lived next door to each other when we were young.*

Language study

1 Read the magazine article quickly. What do you think the interviewer asked the interviewees?

When did you meet your partner?
What's your favourite romantic memory?
When did you first fall in love?

2 Read the texts. In the first text, choose the correct alternative. In the second text, use the correct form of the words in the box.

3 36 Listen and check your answers to Ex 2.

accountant

For my 21st birthday my boyfriend bought me (1) *a / an* expensive-looking box. I (2) *open / opened* it, and there (3) *was / were* a beautiful ring and (4) *an / some* earrings. He picked (5) *me / my* up from work and we (6) *went / are* going to the mountains in his car. He had (7) *a / some* food in a picnic basket and he gave me the present after (8) *a / some* romantic picnic for two. I (9) *can / can't* think of a more wonderful day!

Piotr Nowak, film maker

go	have	live	make	not go	not phone	visit

I enjoy (1) _________ new places and I (2) _________ to India for three months before going to university. My girlfriend (3) _________ with me. I (4) _________ a lot of phonecalls to her, but she (5) _________ me back. I thought she was angry with me. When I got to the airport in Warsaw she was there. And she (6) _________ a big sign in her hands. It said, 'I can't (7) _________ without you!'.

Vocabulary

1 Work in teams of two or three players.
Read the rules and play 'Word relations'.

Word relations

HOW TO PLAY

Each team needs two dice.

1. The starting team throws the two dice. They call out the numbers.
2. Look at the words in the columns with the same numbers as your dice.
   Choose one word from each column. Call out the two words.
3. You have 30 seconds to make a sentence using the two words.
   You can change the form of the words.
   Example: **aunt make** *My aunt made a chocolate cake for my birthday.*
4. The other teams listen and decide if the sentence is correct.
5. Cross out the words in the columns as the teams use them. The words can't be used by other teams.

SCORE

If you use both words in a correct sentence: **5 points**
If you use one word only in a correct sentence: **1 point**
The team with the most points at the end of the game is the winner.

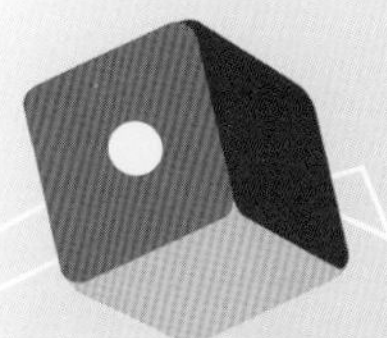					
boots	aunt	dance	behind	cleaning	come
coat	brother	draw	can't stand	cooking	do
hat	cousin	go for a walk	enjoy	drive a car	drop
jacket	daughter	go to the gym	in	gardening	eat
jeans	father	go to the theatre	in front of	hairdresser	go
jumper	grandchildren	go out	next to	housework	hate
scarf	grandparents	listen to music	on	ironing	have
shirt	mother	play a musical instrument	pick up	mechanic	like
shoes	nephew	play video games	put down	nurse	look
skirt	niece	read	put on	secretary	love
tie	parents	send text messages	throw away	shopping	make
top	sister	sing	turn off	sweep the floor	not mind
trainers	son	swim	turn on	take out the rubbish	open
trousers	uncle	take photos	under	washing clothes	prefer
belt	family	watch DVDs	wash up	work	start

Song

1 Read the factfile about Franz Ferdinand and answer the questions.

1 How many people are there in the band?
2 Where did they practise at first?
3 When did they make their first single?
4 Is the band popular in the United States?

factfile

Franz Ferdinand are a rock band from Glasgow, Scotland. They took their name from a famous Austro-Hungarian Archduke. His murder in Sarajevo in 1914 started World War I. At the end of 2001 Bob Hardy (bass guitar), Alex Kapranos (singer/guitar) and Mick McCarthy (guitar) started working on music together. The group played in McCarthy's house, then they started playing with Paul Thomson (drums) and *Franz Ferdinand* was born.
The band began practising in an old warehouse in Glasgow. They called it *The chateau* and they had rave-like parties there. After a while the police stopped the parties, but *Franz Ferdinand* was already a popular band in the city.
The band signed to the Domino record label in the summer of 2003 and released their first single in the same year. They released their first album, *Franz Ferdinand*, in February 2004. It was an immediate success in both Britain and the United States. The song *Tell her tonight* is from this album.

2 **37** Listen to the song and choose the correct alternative.

Tell her tonight

I only watched her ***talk / walk / laugh*** but she saw it
I only heard her ***talk / walk / laugh*** but she saw it
I only touched her ***back / hand / lips*** but she saw it
I only kissed her ***hair / lips / mouth*** but she saw it

Gonna* have to tell her tonight …

She only blinked her ***hands / ears / eyes*** but I saw it
She only swung her ***hair / head / arms*** but I saw it
She only shook her ***head / hips / hands*** but I saw it
She only licked her ***lips / fingers / nose*** but I saw it

Gonna have to tell her tonight …

I only watched her ***talk / walk / laugh*** but she saw it
I only heard her ***talk / walk / laugh*** but she saw it
I only touched her ***back / hand / hips*** but she saw it
I only kissed her ***hair / lips / mouth*** but she saw it

Gonna have to tell her tonight …

Glossary Gonna* = going to

3 Read and listen to the song again. Choose the best answer.

1 The song is about the ___________ of a relationship.
  a beginning b middle c end

2 The woman sees the singer's ___________.
  a girlfriend b new car c feelings for her

3 The singer wants to say ___________ to the woman.
  a 'I don't like you.' b 'Do you like me?' c 'I love you!'

4 Discuss these questions.

1 Do you think *Tell her tonight* is a romantic song?
2 What's your favourite love song? When did you first hear it?
3 Do you believe in love at first sight?

Speaking: housemates debate

The situation

You are a group of friends. You share a house together. But too many people live in the house and you need to throw one person out.

Step 1: Creating characters

1 Work in groups. You are going to invent characters for the housemates. Complete a character profile for your invented person in column 1.

	1	2
Name:		
Age:		
Special abilities: • sports • languages • housework skills • talents (sing, play music, etc.)		
Likes:		
Dislikes:		

2 Why is it important that you stay in the house? Invent reasons.

Example: *I can cook very nice food. I like being with people. I don't like listening to loud music.*

Step 2: Exchanging information

3 Interview a partner from your group to find out all about him or her. Complete column 2 with his / her details.

4 Write two reasons why you want your partner to leave the house.

Example: *He loves watching TV and can't live for a day without watching it. He can't cook.*

Step 3: The debate

5 Work in your groups. Decide who's leaving the house. Use the phrases in the box to help you.

- Present your reasons for staying in the house.
- Explain why you want your partner to go.
- When other students are speaking you can ask questions and make comments.
- Decide who's leaving the house.

That's not true. What do you mean? What do you think? I think …
I agree. I don't agree.

6 Explain your choice to other groups.

Extra practice

Unit 1

1 Find 17 words for colours and clothes in this wordsearch. Write two lists.

S	B	I	A	T	S	H	I	R	T
K	R	B	G	R	E	E	N	D	I
I	A	X	I	O	R	A	N	G	E
R	E	D	J	U	M	P	E	R	D
T	O	P	C	S	A	H	O	E	B
W	H	I	T	E	G	A	S	Y	O
I	S	C	A	R	F	T	H	E	O
T	W	O	I	S	R	C	O	A	T
Y	E	L	L	O	W	G	E	M	S
T	R	A	I	N	E	R	S	Y	N

2 Look at the table and complete the sentences.

Can you ... ?	Sandra	Andy
Ciao	✓	✗
	✓	✗
	✗	✓
	✓	✓
	✗	✗

1 Sandra ___________ speak Italian but Andy ___________.

2 Andy ___________ play the guitar but Sandra ___________.

3 Andy ___________ drive and cook.

4 Sandra and Andy ___________ both cook.

5 Sandra ___________ drive or ride a motorbike.

3 Complete these sentences with *can* or *can't* and a verb from the box.

drive eat go out read see understand

1 He speaks too fast and I ___________ him.

2 I ___________ on Sunday because I've got an exam on Monday.

3 He ___________ a car but he doesn't enjoy it.

4 I ___________ newspapers in French, but I don't understand the news on TV.

5 I'm sorry, but I ___________ anything; I'm not feeling very well.

6 I think you need glasses; you ___________ anything!

4 Put the dialogue in the correct order.

B: Yes, I like those. Can I try them on? ☐

A: Of course. Just a minute … ☐

B: Yes, please. I'm looking for a pair of smart shoes. ☐

A: Here you are … Size 9½. ☐

B: These are perfect. How much are they? ☐

A: How about these black ones? ☐

B: Can I pay by credit card? ☐

A: Hello. Can I help you? *1*

B: Oh, dear. They're a bit too small. Can I try a size 10? ☐

A: Yes, of course. What size are you? ☐

A: Fifty-nine pounds and ninety-nine pence. ☐

B: Size 9½. ☐

A: Yes, you can. Sign here, please. ☐

Unit 2

1 Look at the family tree and correct the sentences.

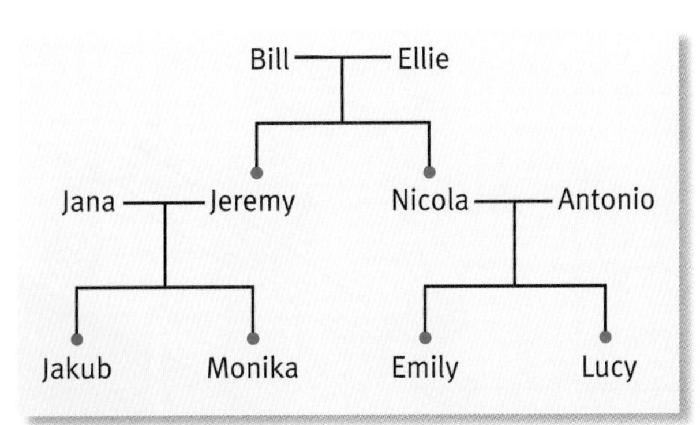

Example:
Bill is Nicola's *father.*

1 Emily is Antonio's ____________
2 Bill is Lucy's ____________
3 Monika is Emily's ____________
4 Jana is Lucy's ____________
5 Jeremy is Jana's ____________
6 Jakub is Jana's ____________
7 Emily is Jana's ____________

2 Complete the sentences using the words and phrases in the box.

divorced	live together	married	retired	see each other

1 'Are you ________?' 'Yes, I am. My husband's name is Sam.'
2 My grandfather doesn't work now. He's ________.
3 My brother and his girlfriend aren't married but they ________.
4 Her parents are ________, and she lives with her mother during the week and her father at weekends.
5 My cousin and I don't ________ very often because she lives in Poland.

3 Rearrange the jumbled letters to make free time activities.

1 I can't *nisg* or *wrad* but I can *cadne* well.
________, ________, ________
2 My brother *laysp edovi smage* all the time.
____
3 My sister doesn't often *chawt VT* but she always *stensil ot smiuc.* ________, ________
4 My dad *soge ot het mgy* twice a week and *sojg* every morning. ________, ________
5 Rick *egso tou* about twice a week to *evah* a *knidr* with his friends. ________, ________

4 Complete the interview with the words in the box.

can't stand
doing
don't like
don't mind
going
like
love
prefer
reading

Interviewer: What do you (1) ________ doing in your free time?
Amelie: Well, I really (2) ________ watching MTV. That's my favourite thing. I also like (3) ________ books, but my boyfriend doesn't.
Carlos: That's right. I (4) ________ reading much. I (5) ________ going to the gym instead.
Interviewer: Do you like (6) ________ to the gym, Amelie?
Amelie: I (7) ________ it. I mean, it's OK – but it isn't my favourite thing.
Interviewer: And is there something that you really hate (8) ________ in your free time?
Amelie: Yes, there is. I (9) ________ jogging!

5 Write true sentences about your and your family's likes and dislikes.

1 I ____________
(go for long walks)
2 My ____________
(spend New Year's Eve with my family)
3 I ____________
(watch football matches)
4 My ____________
(dance)
5 I ____________
(go to the theatre)
6 My ____________
(go for drives in fast cars)

6 What is the *'s* in these sentences? Tick (✓) the correct column.

		is	*has*	possessive *'s*
1	He's got a girlfriend.	☐	☐	☐
2	Ellie's very tall.	☐	☐	☐
3	They're Julie's trainers.	☐	☐	☐
4	Have you got any children's jumpers?	☐	☐	☐
5	It's my favourite top.	☐	☐	☐
6	What's he got in his hand?	☐	☐	☐

Unit 3

1 Look at the picture. Complete the sentences with the correct prepositions of place.

behind	in	in front of	next to	on	under

1 The *Gone with the wind* poster is ____________ the clock.

2 You can buy *Apocalypse now* posters. They're ____________ a box ____________ the desk.

3 The *Casablanca* poster is ____________ the desk.

4 There's a *Some like it hot* poster ____________ the wall, ____________ the *Amelie* poster.

2 Replace the underlined words with a pronoun from the box.

her	him	it	it	them	us	them

1 Can we throw this old suitcase away?

____

2 Put your sister down.

____

3 Turn the computer on, please.

____

4 He can pick my brother and me up at the same time.

____

5 Can you wash the breakfast things up, please?

____

6 Put your boots on.

____

7 I'm meeting Michael's father at 2 o'clock.

____

3 Are these countable or uncountable nouns? Write *C* (Countable) or *U* (Uncountable).

1 shoe
2 trousers
3 money
4 table
5 furniture
6 apple
7 beer
8 music
9 guitar
10 computer

4 Complete these sentences with *a* / *an* or *some*.

1 I need ____________ new shoes.
2 Would you like ____________ apple?
3 Let's listen to ____________ music.
4 I haven't got ____________ guitar.
5 They've got ____________ beautiful old furniture.
6 Is there ____________ computer in the classroom?
7 I'd like ____________ water, please.
8 That's ____________ expensive costume.

5 Complete these sentences with *some* or *any*.

1 Has he got ____________ instruments from Africa?
2 There's ____________ really ugly furniture in that new shop.
3 I'm sorry, but I haven't got ____________ money with me. Can I pay you tomorrow?
4 We haven't got ____________ bananas. Can you buy some?
5 There's ____________ water in the fridge.
6 Thank you, but I don't want ____________ beer. I don't drink.

Unit 4

1 Complete the puzzle.

1 My husband does the ____ after every meal.
2 I hate going ____ for clothes.
3 Please take out the ____; it smells terrible.
4 I make the ____ before breakfast every morning.
5 The house gets dirty very quickly; so we do the ____ every Saturday.
6 I can't do the ____ because the machine doesn't work.
7 I need to ____ my shirt for tomorrow.
8 Ayesha is outside doing the ____.
9 Marc is doing the ____ in the kitchen.

1			H						
2			O						
	3		U						
4			S						
5			E						
		6	W						
7			O						
8			R						
9			K						

2 Underline the verbs in the sentences and mark them *R* (regular) or *I* (irregular).

Example:
Jon drops his children at school on his way to work. *R*

1 He starts work at 9 o'clock.
2 He looks at emails first thing.
3 He makes himself a coffee at 11 o'clock.
4 He opens his letters and cards after coffee.
5 He has lunch at 1 o'clock.
6 He goes back to work at 2 o'clock.
7 He does the housework in the evening.

3 Rewrite the sentences in Ex 2 in the past simple to describe Jon's day yesterday.

4 Read about Amy Johnson. Complete the text using the past simple form of the verbs.

AMY JOHNSON

(1903–1941)

Amy Johnson's family (1 come) *came* from Hull in the north-east of England. Amy (2 be) ______ very good at Science at school and (3 love) ________ sports. Most women (4 not / go) ________ to university at that time but Amy (5 go) ________ to the University of Sheffield to study Economics.

After university, Amy (6 move) ________ to London. She didn't get a job in Economics because she (7 be) ________ a woman – so she (8 work) ________ as a secretary. Amy was bored with her job and she (9 want) ________ to do something exciting. She (10 start) ______ flying planes in 1928 and by 1929 she (11 have) ______ her pilot's licence.

Amy was a famous pilot. In 1930 she flew about 11,000 miles* from England to Australia in nineteen and a half days. She died in 1941 when she (12 have) ______ a plane crash in London.

*11,000 miles = 17,700 kilometres

5 Correct the sentences about Amy Johnson.

Example:
Amy's family came from Australia.
Amy's family didn't come from Australia, they came from England.

1 Amy was good at Art at school.
____
2 She went to university in London.
____
3 She thought her job was exciting.
____
4 She started flying in 1930.
____
5 She flew from England to India in 1930.
____

Grammar reference

Unit 1

Talking about ability: *can / can't*

Positive and negative

I You He/She/It We They	can can't	swim.

Questions			Short answers
Can	you he they	swim?	Yes, I can. No, they can't.

can and *can't* are the same for all persons.
He ***can*** *draw.* NOT ~~*He cans draw.*~~

You use the infinitive without *to* after *can* and *can't*.
She ***can*** *speak three languages.*

You don't use *Do* or *Does* to make questions.
Can *you hear me?* NOT ~~*Do you can hear me?*~~

Use

You often use *can* and *can't* to express ability or inability to do something.

I ***can*** *take good photos.*
I ***can't*** *draw.*

Personal pronouns and possessive adjectives

Subject pronouns	Object pronouns	Possesive adjectives
I	me	my
you	you	your
he	him	his
she	her	her
it	it	its
we	us	our
they	them	their

I *like black.*
Black clothes suit ***me****.*
My *favourite colour is black.*

Unit 2

Expressing likes and dislikes

You can express likes, dislikes and preferences with these verbs.

Negative	Neutral	Positive
hate	don't mind	love
don't like		like
can't stand		enjoy
		prefer

After these verbs we use verb + *-ing*.
I prefer ***staying*** *in London.*
They don't like ***seeing*** *each other.*
Does he like ***looking after*** *his brother?*

In regular verbs ending in short vowel + consonant, the last consonant is doubled.

Why do you hate ***shopping****?*

Use of *'s*

Possession

You use *'s* to express belonging or possession:
*My sister****'s*** *name is Harriet.*
*Jasper****'s*** *house is in London.*

You use *'s* to show relationships:
*Tom****'s*** *mother lives in the country.*

In short forms

You also use *'s* as a short form of the verbs *be* and *have (got)*.
*He****'s*** *in his mid-twenties. = He is in his mid-twenties.*
*She****'s*** *got two children. = She has got two children.*

Unit 3

Countable and uncountable nouns

There are two groups of nouns; those you can count (countable) and those you can't count (uncountable).

Countable nouns can be singular or plural.

Countable nouns

bed	singular: *Our house is in Prague.*
house	or
banana	plural: *These bananas are bad.*
can of beer	

We only use singular verb forms with uncountable nouns.

Uncountable nouns

beer	are always singular:
food	*This beer is good.*
money	*Your money is on the table.*
furniture	

a / an and *some / any*

You use *a / an* and *some / any* to talk about the quantity of something. You use *a / an* with singular countable nouns. You use *some / any* with plural, countable nouns and with uncountable nouns.

Nouns	*a / an*	*some / any*
singular, countable	✓	✗
plural, countable	✗	✓
uncountable	✗	✓

There's ***a*** *large collection in the house.*
I haven't got ***an*** *apple.*
He's got ***some*** *cans.*
There aren't ***any*** *French labels.*
Have you got ***any*** *children?*

You use *some* in positive sentences.
He's got ***some*** *fantastic photos.*

You use *any* in negative sentences.
They don't have ***any*** *money.*

You usually use *any* in questions.
Have you got ***any*** *Franz Ferdinand CDs?*

But, you use *some* in questions when we make **requests** or **offers**.
Can I have ***some*** *beer?*
Would you like ***some*** *bananas?*

Unit 4

Talking about the past

The past simple

Regular verbs

With regular verbs you form the past simple tense in the following ways:

+ *-ed*
Most verbs add *-ed* to the infinitive form:
ask → asked *happen → happened* *start → started*

+ *-ied*
Verbs that end in consonant + *-y*:
study → studied

+ *-d*
Verbs that end in consonant + *-e*:
hate → hated

Verbs ending in a short vowel + consonant
For these verbs, the last consonant is doubled:
drop → dropped *shop → shopped*

Irregular verbs

These are the past simple forms of some common irregular verbs in English.

come → came	*make → made*
do → did	*say → said*
drive → drove	*send → sent*
eat → ate	*take → took*
fly → flew	*think → thought*
get → got	*understand → understood*
go → went	*tell → told*
have → had	*write → wrote*
know → knew	

Positive and negative

I / you he / she / it we / they	start**ed** **didn't start** (regular verb) **went** **didn't go** (irregular verb)	at six o'clock.

Questions

Did	I / you / he / she / it / we / they	**visit** Mum and Dad last weekend? **have** dinner late yesterday?

be

The verb *be* is the only verb in the English language with two forms in the past simple (was/were).

Positive and negative

I / he / she / it	was wasn't	at home.
you / we / they	were weren't	

Questions			Short answers
Was	I / he / she / it	at home?	Yes, I / he / she / it was.
			No, I / he / she / it wasn't.
Were	you / we / they		Yes, you / we / they were.
			No, you / we / they weren't.

Use

We use the past simple for actions in the past that are finished. We often use the past simple with a past time phrase (for example, ***yesterday, last week, at 2 o'clock***).

Wordlist

*** the 2,500 most common English words, ** very common words, * fairly common words

Unit 1
a bit *adv* /ə ˈbɪt/ ***
bend down *v* /ˌbend ˈdaʊn/
black *adj* /blæk/ ***
blue *adj* /bluː/ ***
boot *n* /buːt/ ***
brown *adj* /braʊn/ ***
car *n* /kɑː/ ***
casual *adj* /ˈkæʒuəl/ **
changing room *n* /ˈtʃeɪndʒɪŋ ˌruːm/
coat *n* /kəʊt/ ***
comfortably *adv* /ˈkʌmftəbli/ ***
cook *v* /kʊk/ ***
credit card *n* /ˈkredɪt ˌkɑːd/ **
dark *adj* /dɑːk/ ***
dark-coloured *adj* /ˌdɑːk ˌkʌləd/
doorbell *n* /ˈdɔːˌbel/
draw *v* /drɔː/ ***
dress *n* /dres/ ***
drive *v* /draɪv/ ***
earring *n* /ˈɪərɪŋ/ *
(not) ... enough *adv* /(ˌnɒt) ˈː ɪˌnʌf/ ***
good on (you) *phrase* /ˈgʊd ɒn ˌ(juː)/
green *adj* /griːn/ ***
grey *adj* /greɪ/ ***
hat *n* /hæt/ ***
height *n* /haɪt/ ***
help *v* /help/ ***
here you are *phrase* /ˈhɪə juː ˌɑː/
How much is ...? *phrase* /ˈhaʊ ˌmʌtʃ ɪz ˌ.../
jacket *n* /ˈdʒækɪt/ ***
jeans *n* /dʒiːnz/ *
jumper *n* /ˈdʒʌmpə/ *
lift *n* /lɪft/ **
light *adj* /laɪt/ ***
long *adj* /lɒŋ/ ***
look for *v* /ˈlʊk ˌfɔː, fə/
low *adj* /ləʊ/ ***
motorbike *n* /ˈməʊtəˌbaɪk/ *
musical instrument *n* /ˌmjuːzɪkl ˈɪnstrʊmənt/
nice *adj* /naɪs/ ***
orange *adj* /ˈɒrɪndʒ/ **
pink *adj* /pɪŋk/ **
place *n* /pleɪs/ ***
play *v* /pleɪ/ ***
please *expr* /pliːz/ ***
pretty *adj* /ˈprɪti/ **
public *adj* /ˈpʌblɪk/ ***
purple *adj* /ˈpɜːpl/ *
reach *v* /riːtʃ/ ***
red *adj* /red/ ***
ride *v* /raɪd/ ***
scarf *n* /skɑːf/ *
shirt *n* /ʃɜːt/ ***
shoe *n* /ʃuː/ ***
short *adj* /ʃɔːt/ ***
sing *v* /sɪŋ/ ***
size *n* /saɪz/ ***
skirt *n* /skɜːt/ **
smart *adj* /smɑːt/ **
snowboard *v* /ˈsnəʊbɔːd/
stand up *v* /ˌstænd ˈʌp/
straight *adj* /streɪt/ **
suit *n, v* /suːt/ ***
swim *v* /swɪm/ **
take photos *phrase* /ˌteɪk ˈfəʊtəʊz/
tall *adj* /tɔːl/ ***
tie *n* /taɪ/ **
too *adv* /tuː/ ***
top *n* /tɒp/ ***
trainer *n* /ˈtreɪnə/ ***
transport *n* /ˈtrænspɔːt/ ***
trousers *n* /ˈtraʊzəz/ **
try sth on *phrase* /ˌtraɪ ... ˈɒn/
Turkish *n, adj* /ˈtɜːkɪʃ/
waistcoat *n* /ˈweɪstˌkəʊt/
wedding *n* /ˈwedɪŋ/ ***
white *adj* /waɪt/ ***
yellow *adj* /ˈjeləʊ/ ***

Unit 2
aunt *n* /ɑːnt/ ***
bank account *n* /ˈbæŋk əˌkaʊnt/ *
boyfriend *n* /ˈbɔɪˌfrend/ **
brother *n* /ˈbrʌðə/ ***
buy *v* /baɪ/ ***
can't stand *phrase* /ˌkɑːnt ˈstænd/
clothes *n* /kləʊðz/ ***
cousin *n* /ˈkʌzn/ **
dancing *n* /ˈdɑːnsɪŋ/ *
daughter *n* /ˈdɔːtə/ ***
divorced *adj* /dɪˈvɔːst/ **
each other *pron* /ˌiːtʃ ˈʌðə/ **
early *adj* /ˈɜːli/ ***
enjoy *v* /ɪnˈdʒɔɪ/ ***
every (15 minutes) *phrase* /ˌevri (ˌfɪftiːn ˈmɪnɪts)/ ***
exam *n* /ɪgˈzæm/ **
fall in love *phrase* /ˌfɔːl ɪn ˈlʌv/
father *n* /ˈfɑːðə/ ***
fly *v* /flaɪ/ ***
get a job *phrase* /ˌget ə ˈdʒɒb/
get married *phrase* /ˌget ˈmærɪd/
girlfriend *n* /ˈgɜːlˌfrend/ **
grandchildren *n* /ˈgrænˌtʃɪldrən/
grandfather *n* /ˈgrænˌfɑːðə/ **
grandmother *n* /ˈgrænˌmʌðə/ **
grandparent *n* /ˈgrænˌpeərənt/ *
gym *n* /dʒɪm/ *
half brother *n* /ˈhɑːf ˌbrʌðə/
hate *v* /heɪt/ ***
house *n* /haʊs/ ***
jogging *n* /ˈdʒɒgɪŋ/ *
late *adj* /leɪt/ ***
less than *phrase* /ˈles ðən/ ***
like *v* /laɪk/ ***
live together *phrase* /ˈlɪv təˌgeðə/
look after *v* /ˌlʊk ˈɑːftə/
love *v* /lʌv/ ***
mid *adj* /mɪd/
most *det* /məʊst/ ***
mother *n* /ˈmʌðə/ ***
nephew *n* /ˈnefjuː/ *
niece *n* /niːs/ *
(not) mind *v* /(ˌnɒt) ˈmaɪnd/ ***
once (a year) *adv* /ˌwʌns (ə ˈjɪə)/ ***
open *v* /ˈəʊpən/ ***
parents *n* /ˈpeərənts/ ***
part-time *adj* /ˌpɑːt ˈtaɪm/ **
pop concert *n* /ˈpɒp ˌkɒnsət/
prefer *v* /prɪˈfɜː/ ***
put on weight *phrase* /ˌpʊt ɒn ˈweɪt/
retire *v* /rɪˈtaɪə/ **
retired *adj* /rɪˈtaɪəd/ *
sister *n* /ˈsɪstə/ ***
son *n* /sʌn/ ***
sports car *n* /ˈspɔːts ˌkɑː/
stay *v* /steɪ/ ***
teens *n* /tiːnz/
(three or four) times (a week) *phrase* /(ˌθriː ɔː ˌfɔː) ˌtaɪmz ə (ˈwiːk)/ ***
twenties *n* /ˈtwentiz/
twice (a month) *adv* /ˌtwaɪs ə (ˈmʌnθ)/ ***
uncle *n* /ˈʌŋkl/ **
video game *n* /ˈvɪdiəʊ ˌgeɪm/ *
walk *n* /wɔːk/ ***
wife *n* /waɪf/ ***

Unit 3
(home) computer *n* /(ˌhəʊm) kəmˈpjuːtə/ ***
beer can *n* /ˈbɪə ˌkæn/
behind *prep* /bɪˈhaɪnd/ ***
check *v* /tʃek/ ***
clutter *n* /ˈklʌtə/
collection *n* /kəˈlekʃn/ ***
dirty *adj* /ˈdɜːti/ **
drum *n* /drʌm/ **
forget *v* /fəˈget/ ***
free time *n* /ˌfriː ˈtaɪm/
go to bed *phrase* /ˌgəʊ tə ˈbed/
house *n* /haʊs/ ***
important *adj* /ɪmˈpɔːtnt/ ***
in front of *prep* /ˌɪn ˈfrʌnt əv/ ***
in *prep* /ɪn/ ***
insane *adj* /ɪnˈseɪn/
journey *n* /ˈdʒɜːni/ ***
keep *v* /kiːp/ ***
kitchen *n* /ˈkɪtʃən/ ***
label *n* /ˈleɪbl/ **
leave *v* /liːv/ ***
marble *n* /ˈmɑːbl/ *
neighbour *n* /ˈneɪbə/ ***
next to *prep* /ˈnekst tə/ ***
obsessed *adj* /əbˈsest/ *
obsessive *adj* /əbˈsesɪv/
occasion *n* /əˈkeɪʒn/ ***
on *prep* /ɒn/ ***
pick sth up *v* /ˌpɪk ... ˈʌp/
plate *n* /pleɪt/ ***
put sth down *v* /ˌpʊt ... ˈdaʊn/
put sth on *v* /ˌpʊt ... ˈɒn/
remember *v* /rɪˈmembə/ ***
throw sth away *v* /ˌθrəʊ ... əˈweɪ/ ***
tidy *adj* /ˈtaɪdi/ *
tomorrow *adv* /təˈmɒrəʊ/ ***
turn sth off *v* /ˌtɜːn ... ˈɒf/
turn sth on *v* /ˌtɜːn ... ˈɒn/
under *prep* /ˈʌndə/ ***
valuable *adj* /ˈvæljʊbl/ ***
worth *n, adj* /wɜːθ/ ***

Unit 4
accountant *n* /əˈkaʊntənt/ **
ballet dancer *n* /ˈbæleɪ ˌdɑːnsə/
chef *n* /ʃef/ *
chore *n* /tʃɔː/
do the cleaning *phrase* /ˌduː ðə ˈkliːnɪŋ/
do the cooking *phrase* /ˌduː ðə ˈkʊkɪŋ/
do the gardening *phrase* /ˌduː ðə ˈgɑːdnɪŋ/
do the ironing *phrase* /ˌduː ði ˈaɪənɪŋ/
do the shopping *phrase* /ˌduː ðə ˈʃɒpɪŋ/
do the washing *phrase* /ˌduː ðə ˈwɒʃɪŋ/
do the washing up *phrase* /ˌduː ðə ˌwɒʃɪŋ ˈʌp/
editor *n* /ˈedɪtə/ ***
equally *adv* /ˈiːkwəli/ ***
footballer *n* /ˈfʊtbɔːlə/
hairdresser *n* /ˈheədresə/ *
housework *n* /ˈhaʊswɜːk/ *
husband *n* /ˈhʌzbənd/ ***
make the beds *phrase* /ˌmeɪk ðə ˈbedz/
mechanic *n* /mɪˈkænɪk/ *
nurse *n* /nɜːs/ ***
pilot *n* /ˈpaɪlət/ ***
politician *n* /ˌpɒləˈtɪʃn/ ***
racing driver *n* /ˈreɪsɪŋ ˌdraɪvə/
secretary *n* /ˈsekrətri/ ***
share *v* /ʃeə/ ***
soldier *n* /ˈsəʊldʒə/ ***
strike *v* /straɪk/ ***
sweep the floor *phrase* /ˌswiːp ðə ˈflɔː/
take out the rubbish *phrase* /ˌteɪk ˌaʊt ðə ˈrʌbɪʃ/

Communication activities

Student A

Unit 1, Listening and speaking Ex 4 page 37

Read the rolecard and choose one of the alternatives.

Useful words and phrases
I'm looking for …
a bit too small / big
not large enough

Rolecard

You want to buy some new clothes to wear *to your boyfriend's or girlfriend's birthday party / for a job interview / on holiday*. You have got *£60 / £150 / £250* pounds to spend.

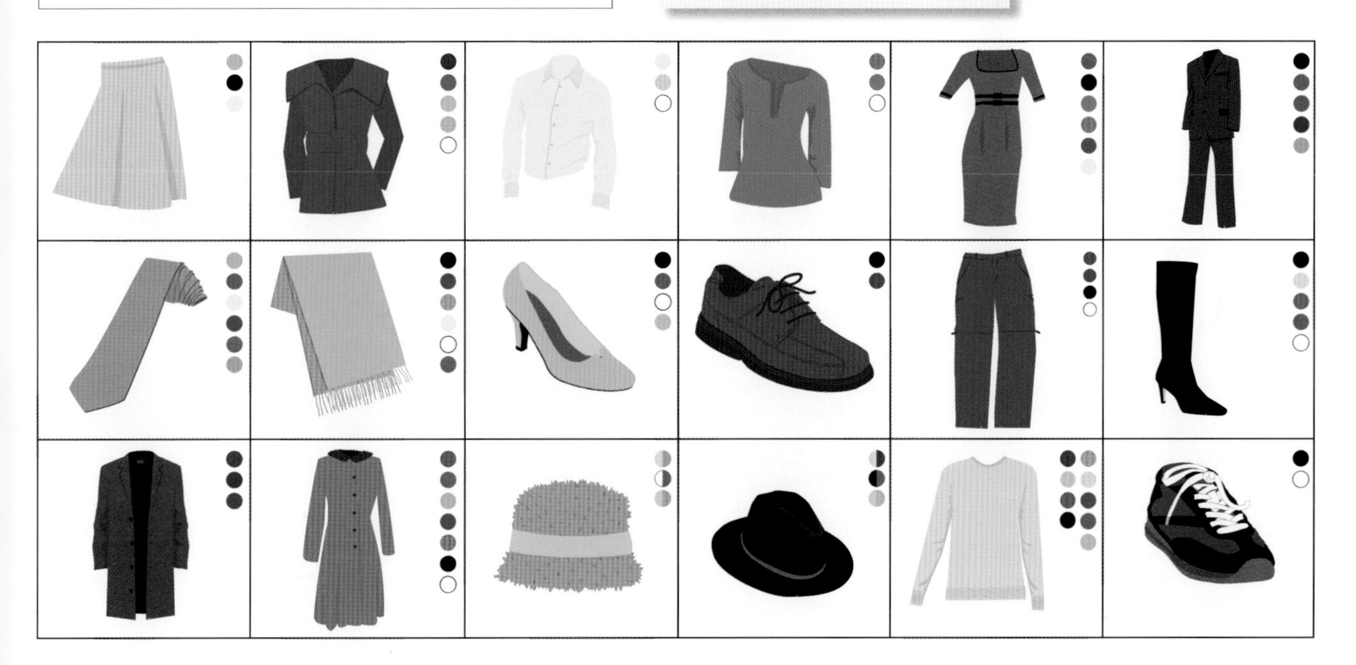

Unit 3, Language study Ex 5 page 44

Look carefully at the picture and try to remember the details. You have one minute.
Think about:

- where the objects are.
- what colour and size the objects are.
- how many things there are.

Listening scripts

Unit 1 Being different

Listening script 21

Reading texts from pages 34 and 35

Listening script 22

Pronunciation Ex 1 from page 35

Listening script 23

Well, I'm learning Turkish, but I can't speak it very well. I can speak English and a little Italian. I love listening to music but I can't play a musical instrument and I can't sing either. I'm quite sporty – I run every morning and I run the London marathon every year – and I can swim. I swim about a kilometre every week. I love skiing and I can ski pretty well, but I can't snowboard. I want to learn this winter. What else can I do? Well, I can ride a motorbike but I can't drive a car. I love cooking and people tell me I'm a very good cook. I can't draw at all – my drawings are really terrible, but my photos are usually very good.

Listening script 24

(A = shop assistant, B = customer)

A: Good morning. Can I help you?
B: Yes, please. I'm looking for something to wear to a wedding.
A: How about a skirt and top?
B: Oh, yes. I love these. Can I try them on?
A: Of course. The changing room's over there.
B: Excuse me. The skirt's a bit small. Have you got a size 14?
A: Yes, here you are.
B: That's perfect. I'll take it, and the top too. And have you got any earrings?
A: Yes, we have. Here you are.
B: Those are pretty. I'll have them too. How much is that?
A: £131.49 please.
B: Can I pay by credit card?
A: Yes, of course.

Unit 2 Family matters

Listening script 25

I go to college – I stay at the college during the week and then go home at weekends.
My mother and father are divorced. I **prefer staying** with my dad because he lives in London. My mum lives in a small village in the country. I **don't mind staying** there in the summer – but in the winter there's nothing to do.
My dad's new wife, Laura, is Spanish. She's fifteen years younger than my father. They've got a one-year-old son, Tom. He's my half brother. I **really enjoy being** with Tom. We have fun together.
My sister Harriet is two years older than me. This year she's in Tanzania with her boyfriend. His family live there. She's working part-time in a school. She **loves being** in Africa, but my dad isn't so happy about it. **He hates being** so far away from her.
My uncle Ian and his wife Jasmin live in Malaysia. They've got one daughter – my cousin Emma. We don't see each other very often because she lives so far away. We're the same age but we're very different. She **doesn't like doing** any sports. She **likes going** shopping and buying clothes. I **can't stand shopping** – it's boring.
My grandmother, Irene, is 92. She lives next door to my father and Laura. She lives on her own because my grandfather, Bert, died in 2004. She doesn't work, of course. She can't walk and she can't see very well. I **love visiting** her because she tells great stories about when she was little, and she has a good sense of humour.

Listening script 26

Reading texts from page 40

Unit 3 Are you crazy?

Listening script 27

Reading text from page 42

Listening script 28

Quiz from page 45

Listening script 29

1 A: Don't close the door. The lights are on in the sitting room.
B: Oh yes. I forgot to turn them off. I'm sorry.

2 A: Lily. Your CDs are all over the floor.
B: Can you pick them up for me? My hands are full.

3 A: There's a good film on tonight. Let's watch TV.
B: I need to write some letters, but you can turn it on if you like.

4 A: This suitcase is heavy. Ooh! Ow!
B: Put it down! It's too heavy for you. I'll take it.

5 A: Those are nice earrings. I can wear them to the party.
B: Great idea. Put them on – you look fantastic.

Listening script 30

(P = Presenter, K = Katie, I = Ian, M = Maggie, S = Sam, B = Bruce)

P: What do you do before you go out in the morning? What do you do for good luck? How do you go to sleep? We all do strange things sometimes. Today in *People everywhere* we talk to some listeners about some of the special little things they do that aren't quite normal.
K: Before I go to work in the morning, I walk all around the house and I touch the doors to all the rooms. I feel terrible when I don't do that. I have a feeling that something terrible is going to happen.
I: For good luck, in an exam for instance, I wear two different socks – one red and one black, for example. Putting on two socks that are the same colour brings me bad luck. I'd fail the exam.
M: When I have an important meeting, or an interview or something, I walk all round the rooms in my house before it, and I say the names of all the people in the photos that I see there. I don't really know why I do it, but I think it brings me good luck.
S: I'm not a good sleeper. Before I go to sleep in the evening, I tidy everything in my bedroom. I put out my clothes for the next day too. When things are untidy, I can't sleep.
B: Before I leave home to go on a long journey, I sit down for about five minutes and say goodbye to the house. Everyone in my family does this – it's for good luck on the journey, but I don't really know why.

Unit 4 Men and women

 Listening script 31

Reading text from page 47

 Listening script 32

Language study Ex 4 from page 48

 Listening script 33

1 What did you have for breakfast?
2 Did you buy anything?
3 How did you go to your class?
4 How many hours did you sleep?
5 Which household chores did you do?
6 What did you do in the evening?

 Listening script 34

I was born in Manchester. It isn't a city famous for dancing exactly, but it's certainly famous for football. My dad was a builder – and he was also a great Manchester United fan. When I started dancing he was so angry – he wanted me to be a builder, too! I started dancing when I was eight. My older sister went to ballet classes and I went with my mum to pick her up and I loved watching the dancing. I played football at school but I hated it. I asked my mum again and again to let me do ballet and in the end she said 'yes'. There were 12 girls in the class and I was the only boy. But I didn't mind. When I was 12 I went to ballet school in London. In countries like Russia it's OK to be a male ballet dancer but here in Britain it's hard. People think it isn't a man's job.

 Listening script 35

I was born in Illinois, in the USA, in 1986. My dad was a chef and my mum was a mechanic. My dad rode a motorbike to work and I loved it. I wanted to race motorbikes when I was little. When I was ten we moved to California. I started racing go-karts there when I was 11. I loved it, and I was good. Then, when I was 16, I decided I wanted to drive cars. My aunt lived in England and I moved here to learn to drive. Europe is the best place for car racing. My family didn't come with me – they stayed in the States. A lot of male drivers have a problem with me. They say that it's easier for me to win because I'm not heavy. That's not really their problem. Their problem is that they don't want to race against a woman!

Unit 5 Review

 Listening script 36

(I = Imogen, P = Piotr)
Imogen Bates, accountant
I: For my 21st birthday my boyfriend bought me an expensive looking box. I opened it, and there was a beautiful ring and some earrings. He picked me up from work and we went to the mountains in his car. He had some food in a picnic basket and he gave me the present after a romantic picnic for two. I don't can't think of a more wonderful day!

Piotr Nowak, film maker
P: I enjoy visiting new places and I went to India for three months before going to university. My girlfriend didn't go with me. I made a lot of phonecalls to her, but she didn't phone me back. I thought she was angry with me. When I got to the airport in Warsaw, she was there. And she had a big sign in her hands. It said, 'I can't live without you!'.

 Listening script 37

Song from page 52

Communication activities

Student B

Unit 1, Listening and speaking Ex 4 page 37

Read the rolecard and follow the instructions.

Useful words and phrases
Can I help you?
How about …?
Yes, of course.
That / These look really nice / pretty / good on you.

Rolecard

You work in a clothes shop. Listen to the customer and suggest clothes in the pictures that he or she can buy. Try to sell as many things as possible.

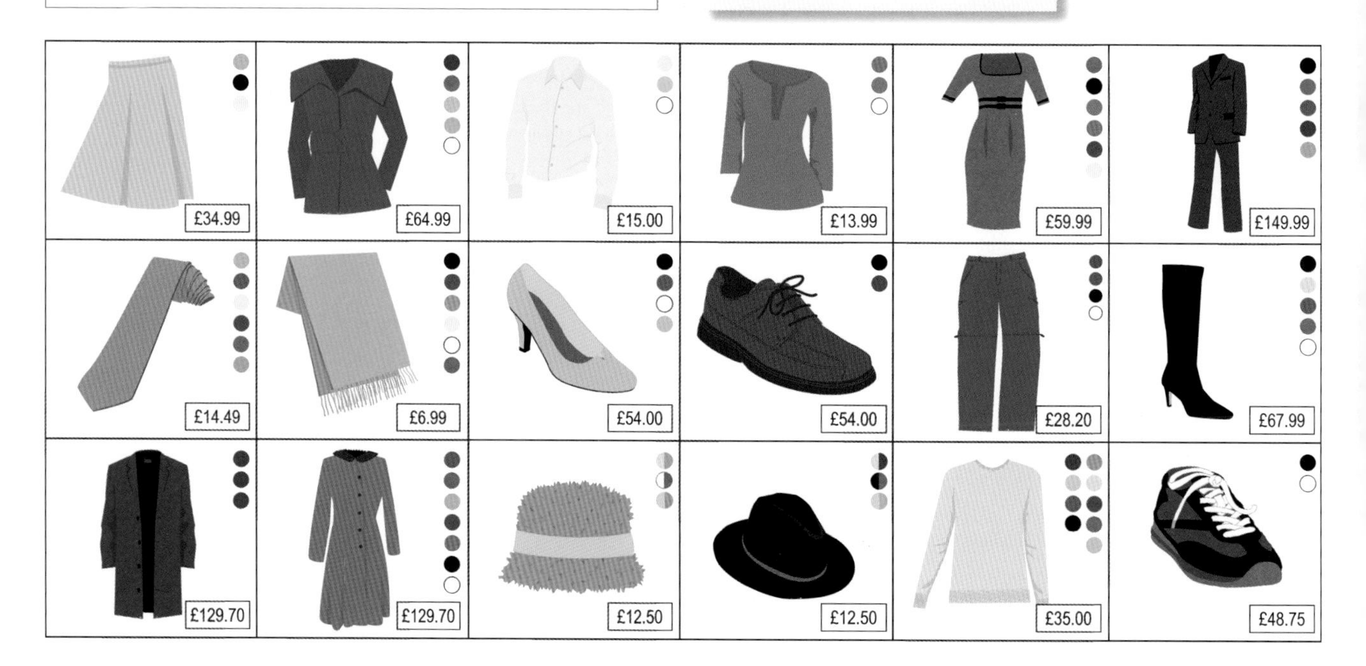

Size conversion chart

Women's sizes

Clothes	UK	8	10	12	14	16	18	20
	Europe	36	38	40	42	44	46	48
	USA	32	34	36	38	40	42	44
Shoes	UK	3	5	5	6	7	8	9
	Europe	36	37	38	39	40	41	42
	USA	5	6	7	8	9	10	11

Men's sizes

Clothes	UK	34	36	38	40	42	44	46
	Europe	44	46	48	50	52	54	56
Shoes	UK	5	6	7	8	9	10	11
	Europe	39	40	41	42	43	44	45
	USA	5.5	6.5	7.5	8.5	9.5	10.5	11.5

Module 3
Choices

nit	Topic	Language study	Vocabulary	Main skills
See the world pages 66–69	• Around the world • On the move (travel and transport)	• Talking about life experiences (the present perfect simple)	• Holiday activities • Words related to travel and transport	• **Reading:** transferring key information • **Pronunciation:** connected speech • **Speaking:** making travel arrangements • **Listening:** identifying the situation in dialogues
Market place pages 70–73	• Buy me! (the power of advertising) • All in a name (well-known companies and their names)	• Comparing things: comparative and superlative adjectives	• Adjectives to describe a product • Business words	• **Listening:** understanding key information • **Reading:** checking predictions • **Speaking:** comparing a variety of products; giving a short presentation
Outdoor life pages 74–77	• Working with the weather (an interview with a weatherman) • What's the weather like?	• Present tenses and future plans (present simple and present continuous for future plans)	• The weather	• **Reading:** understanding main information • **Speaking:** conducting a simple interview; planning a visit to an event • **Listening:** identifying weather conditions
Advances pages 78–81	• Inventions (favourite and least favourite inventions) • Into the future (a chat forum)	• Talking about the future (expressing future intentions with *going to*)	• Modern inventions • Phrasal verbs: discovery and development	• **Listening:** identifying main ideas in a radio programme • **Pronunciation:** diphthongs • **Speaking:** giving and justifying opinions; talking about future plans • **Reading:** understanding and responding to main ideas • **Writing:** an interactive class chat forum

Review unit pages 82–85
Extra practice pages 86–89 • **Grammar reference and wordlist** pages 90–92 • **Listening scripts:** pages 94–95 • **Communication activities:** pages 93, 96
Use CD2 for listening activities in the module

CHOICES

1 See the world

LEARNING AIMS

- Can talk about life experiences
- Can use words related to travel and transport
- Can make travel arrangements

Around the world

Lead-in

1 Which of these activities can you see in the photos?

doing unusual things	eating foreign food	meeting new people	relaxing
sightseeing	sending postcards	shopping for souvenirs	taking photos

2 What do you like and dislike doing on holiday? Work with a partner and compare your ideas.

Example:
A : *What do you like doing on holiday?*
B: *I really like sightseeing, but I can't stand eating foreign food.*

Reading and speaking

1 Which four places in the world would you most like to visit? What would you like to see there? Make a list.

Places to visit	**Things to see**
Egypt	*the Pyramids*
New York	*the Empire State Building*

2 Compare your lists with the class. Does anyone else have the same ideas as you?

3 **01** Read the newspaper article on page 67 about a couple's journey around the world. Why did they see the world in that way? Did they visit any of the places on your list?

4 Read the text again. Number the places on the map in the order Jules and Verne visited them.

5 Make a list of the places they visited and what they did there.

6 Work with a partner. Prepare questions for Jules and Verne about their trip, then ask and answer the questions.

Student A: What …? When …? Where …?
Student B: Who …? Which …? How long …?

Example:
What *did you do in France?*

7 What do you think of Jules and Verne's choice? Do you think it was a good way to use their prize? What do you think life was like for them after the trip?

Around the world in 30 days

Normally Jules (short for Julie) Hollander, 20, and her Canadian husband Verne, 22, work as a waitress and chef in the Havilland Hotel, London. But last month they had a very difficult decision. They won first prize in a magazine competition, and the prize was either £15,000 each or two 30-day airline vouchers and £10,000 spending money. They decided to take time off work and go on a world trip with the vouchers. For a month they've travelled to 12 different locations, and they've done typical things in each place. They've ridden camels in Cairo, and they've been surfing at Sydney's Bondi Beach. From the Colosseum in Rome, to the Grand Bazaar* in Istanbul, they've seen it all. 'Before we started, we got loads of brochures, and worked out our route and travel times,' says Verne. 'Then we booked flights and hotels on the Internet', adds Jules. Their journey began on 2nd October. First came Paris and a magic night at the Moulin Rouge. After that they travelled on to Rome, where they threw coins into the Trevi fountain. 'Our guide explained that tradition to us,' says Verne. 'It mean's you'll go back to Rome some day.' Next they visited Istanbul and Cairo. From there, they flew to Dubai for fruit juice cocktails in the luxurious Burj al Arab hotel. 'That was amazing,' says Jules. Verne's a huge Bollywood movie fan, so in India they visited Mumbai's film studios. 'That was my favourite part of the trip,' he says. 'But I think Jules preferred our moonlight tour of the Taj Mahal.' In Beijing they toured the Forbidden City. 'That was fascinating,' says Jules. Then they visited Tokyo for a delicious sushi* lunch. 'I tried a Japanese breakfast next morning,' says Verne. 'But I didn't really like it'. After that, they flew on to Australia. Their next stop was Buenos Aires, Argentina, where they watched Tango dancers in the streets and enjoyed the exciting nightlife. Next they took a plane to New York for bagels* and coffee in a small café near the Empire State Building. Their final destination was Reykjavik, Iceland, where they relaxed in the Blue Lagoon Spa*. At last, after four weeks' travelling, it was time to go home. Verne says: 'We've certainly had an incredible journey, but we're glad to be back.' Jules adds: 'We've taken great photos and brought back loads of souvenirs – and we've got some really wonderful memories, too!'

Glossary

* Grand Bazaar – big market
* sushi – a Japanese meal of rice with fish and vegetables
* bagel – a small round sweet bread
* spa – a place where water comes from the ground

LANGUAGE STUDY

Talking about life experiences

The present perfect simple

1 Look at this sentence and answer the questions.
Jules has seen the Taj Mahal.

1 Did Jules visit the Taj Mahal on her trip?
2 Do we know exactly when she visited it?
3 Is the sentence about an experience at some point in her life?

2 Choose the correct alternative.

We can use the present perfect to talk about ______.
a finished events at specific times in the past b experiences in our lives in general

3 Read these present perfect sentences and answer the questions.

Have you ever been to Boston?
I've never been to Boston, but I've been to New York.
Verne hasn't been to Boston.

1 Which two verbs are in all of these present perfect sentences?
2 Which one of these verbs is in the past participle form?
3 What do *ever* and *never* mean in the sentences?

Grammar reference page 90

4 **02** Listen and repeat the chant.

Have you ever been to Iceland?
Have you seen the sights in Rome?
Have you flown to California,
or just stayed alone at home?
No, I've never been to Iceland,
California, or Rome.
I've never travelled far away.
I like my life at home.
I've stayed with family and friends,
and never once been bored.
I've seen and done things close to home.
Who needs to go abroad?

5 Underline the past participles in the chant. What are their infinitives?

6 Write the infinitive form of these irregular past participles. Then check your answers in the Grammar reference on page 90.

Example: spent *to spend*

1 bought 2 driven 3 drunk 4 eaten 5 had 6 met 7 ridden 8 sent
9 swum 10 taken

7 Complete these questions, using some of the past participles in Ex 6.

1 Have you ever ____________ underwater photos? ____________
2 Have you ever ____________ foreign food? ____________
3 Have you ever ____________ a foreign boyfriend or girlfriend? ____________
4 Have you ever ____________ in the sea? ____________
5 Have you ever ____________ in a five star hotel? ____________
6 Have you ever ____________ a Bollywood film? ____________

8 Ask and answer the questions in class. For each of the questions, try to find one person in your class who answers *yes*. Write the names.

On the move

Vocabulary and listening

1 Match the words to the numbers.

Railway station | **Bus stop** | **Airport**

Railway station

- ☐ carriage
- ☐ platform
- ☐ ticket inspector
- ☐ ticket office
- ☐ train

Bus stop

- ☐ ticket
- ☐ bus
- ☐ driver
- ☐ passengers
- ☐ seat

Airport

- ☐ boarding card
- ☐ check-in
- ☐ gate
- ☐ plane
- ☐ terminal

2 Complete these sentences with the words in Ex 1.

1. On most London buses now, you buy your __________ from the __________.
2. You get your __________ from the __________ desk. After that, you go to the departure __________.
3. There are five different __________ at London Heathrow airport.
4. Let's ask the man at the __________ which __________ our train leaves from.
5. __________ can choose their own __________ on the bus.

3 03 Listen and match the dialogues to the places.

Railway station	Airport	Bus stop
1		

4 Listen again. Choose the correct alternative in these sentences.

1. A ticket *to* / *for* Oxford, please.
2. Excuse me, is this the right stop *to* / *for* Blackheath?
3. When's *a* / *the* next bus?
4. Which gate does the flight to Warsaw leave *of* / *from*?
5. Is this the right platform for the train *to* / *of* Bristol?
6. When does the train arrive *in* / *to* Bristol?
7. How long *is* / *does* the bus take to get there?
8. Is the plane *in* / *on* time?

5 04 Listen and repeat the phrases in Ex 4.

Speaking

1 Work with a partner. Student A turn to page 93. Student B turn to page 96. Follow the instructions.

CD-ROM For more activities go to **Choices Unit 1**

2 Market place

LEARNING AIMS

- Can use adjectives to describe things
- Can compare a variety of products
- Can describe a product

Buy me!

Lead-in

1 Work with a partner. What things do you buy ...?

- nearly every day
- once a week
- once a month
- once a year, or less often

2 Which things do you like or dislike shopping for? Discuss your ideas.

Speaking and vocabulary

1 Look at the photos from two adverts. Which products are they advertising? Choose from the box.

a car	a digital camera	aftershave	hairspray	a watch	a motorbike
contact lenses	computer software	fish food	sunglasses	perfume	
washing powder					

2 Turn to page 93. Did you guess the products? Do you like the adverts? Why?

3 Think about adverts for famous products. Write the makes of some products with these descriptions.

1 a fast car
2 a perfume with a nice smell
3 a comfortable make of shoes
4 an unusual drink
5 a mobile phone which is easy to use
6 a popular aftershave
7 an expensive watch
8 a fashionable make of clothes
9 a well-known washing powder

4 Underline the adjectives in Ex 3. Match them to their opposites in the box.

Example: fast – *slow*

common	cheap	difficult	horrible
old-fashioned	slow	uncomfortable	
unknown	unpopular		

5 Think of something you have bought recently. Make a list of adjectives to describe it.

6 Talk to as many people as possible in the class. Describe and guess each other's purchases.

Example:

A: *I bought myself something the other day. They're very comfortable. They were quite cheap. They're a well-known make. They're nice but they aren't very fashionable.*

B: *New shoes?*

Listening

1 You want to buy a digital camera. Which of these things are important to you? Choose the three most important. Compare your ideas with a partner.

- It's cheap.
- It looks nice.
- It's a well-known make.
- It's small and light.
- It's got a lot of memory.
- It's easy to use.
- It's got a large screen.
- It takes good pictures.

2 **05** Listen to Tanya talking to a shop assistant and answer the questions.

1. How much does she want to spend?
2. How many cameras does she look at?
3. What does she decide to do in the end?

3 Listen again. Complete the Quick guide to digital cameras.

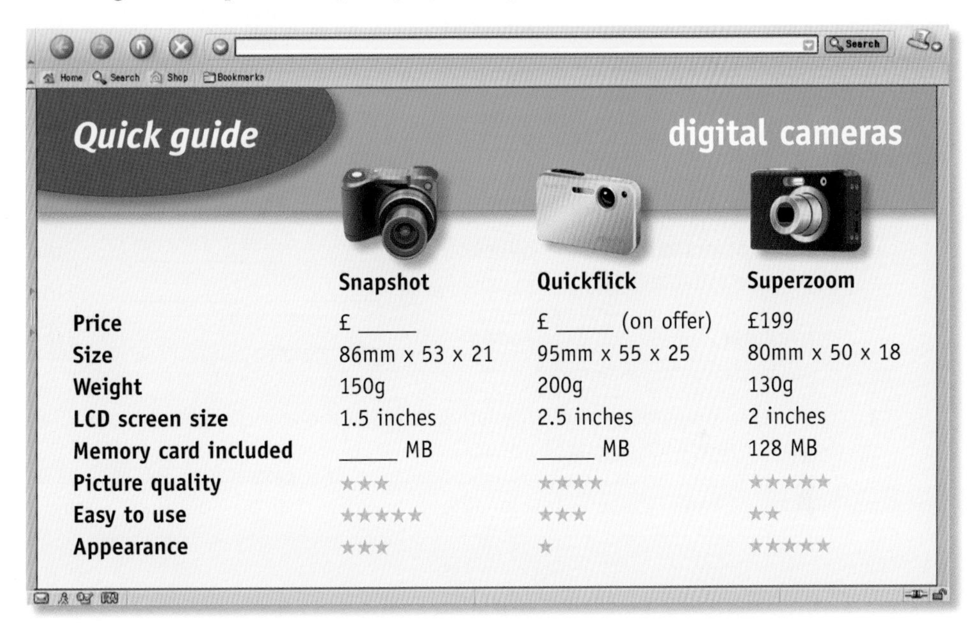

Quick guide **digital cameras**

	Snapshot	Quickflick	Superzoom
Price	£ _____	£ _____ (on offer)	£199
Size	86mm x 53 x 21	95mm x 55 x 25	80mm x 50 x 18
Weight	150g	200g	130g
LCD screen size	1.5 inches	2.5 inches	2 inches
Memory card included	_____ MB	_____ MB	128 MB
Picture quality	★★★	★★★★	★★★★★
Easy to use	★★★★★	★★★	★★
Appearance	★★★	★	★★★★★

4 Use the Quick guide to tick (✓) the columns for the makes of camera.

	Snapshot	Quickflick	Superzoom
1 It's cheaper than the Snapshot.			
2 It's the cheapest.			
3 It's smaller than the Snapshot.			
4 It's heavier than the Snapshot.			
5 It's got the smallest LCD screen.			
6 It's got the largest memory card.			
7 It takes better quality photos than the Quickflick.			
8 It's easier to use than the Quickflick.			
9 It's the most difficult to use.			
10 It's the best-looking camera.			

5 Which of the cameras would you choose? Why?

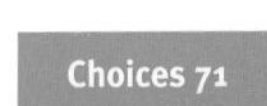

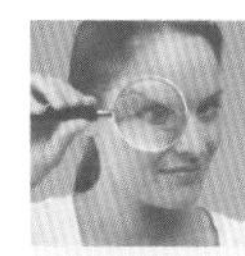

LANGUAGE STUDY

Comparing things

1 Look at these sentences and answer the questions.

Comparatives
The Superzoom is ***smaller than*** *the Snapshot.*
The Snapshot is ***more expensive than*** *the Quickflick.*

Superlatives
The Quickflick is ***the biggest****.*
The Superzoom is ***the most expensive****.*

1 Which sentences are about the difference between two things?
2 Which sentences are about the difference between one thing and the others in a group?

2 Read the spelling rules for comparatives and superlatives and complete the table.

Spelling rules
Short adjectives: most of them add *-er*, *-est*.
Those ending in *-e*: add *-r*, *-st*.
Those ending in a short vowel sound + consonant: double the consonant.
Adjectives ending in *-y*: change change to *-i*, (*-ier*, *-iest*).
Long adjectives: add *more*, *most*.

	Adjective	Comparative	Superlative
Short (one syllable)	cheap large big	______ ______ ______	the ______ the ______ the ______
Adjectives ending in ***-y***	heavy	______	the ______
Long (others with two or more syllables)	difficult expensive	______ ______ ______ ______	the ______ ______ the ______ ______
Irregular	good	______	the ______

3 Guess the comparative and superlative forms of the adjectives in the box. Check your answers in the Grammar reference on pages 90–91.

angry	bad	busy	fashionable	healthy	nice	popular	slow	unusual	useful

Grammar reference pages 90–91

4 Compare the TVs and write sentences.
1 The PH370X and SN21. (big)
2 The PH370X and HW40. (expensive)
3 The HW40 and SN21. (heavy)

Speaking

1 Read these survey questions and add one more. Answer the questions for you, then interview other students.

Which is ...
1 ... the most expensive thing you've ever bought?
2 ... the fastest car you've ever driven, or been in?
3 ... the best meal you've ever eaten?
4 ... the most unusual place you've been on holiday?
5 ... the nicest present you've ever received?
6 ... (your question) ______________________?

2 Choose the most interesting thing you found out and tell the class.

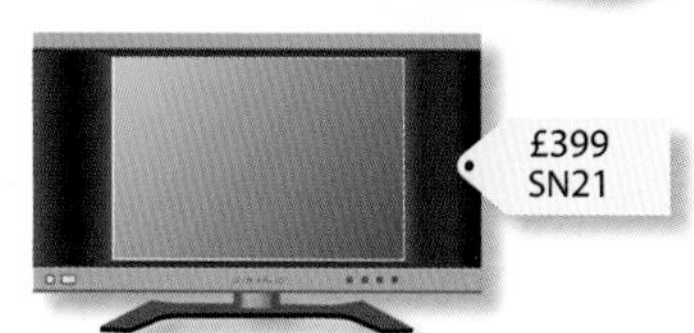

All in a name

Reading and vocabulary

1 What are these six well-known international companies famous for?

Bridgestone	Google	Hyundai	Ikea	Nokia	Reebok

2 **06** Read the article and check your answers in Ex 1.

3 Find words in **bold** in the text which mean:

1. the person who starts a company
2. two words that mean *a company*
3. made something
4. a word for the things a company makes
5. a ___ company makes a lot of money

4 Complete these sentences with the correct form of the words in Ex 3.

1. Michelin, Goodyear and Bridgestone are large tyre __________ .
2. The __________ of Google were Larry Page and Sergay Brin.
3. Hyundai first __________ the Tiburon car in 1996.
4. Ikea founder, Kamprad, first started selling __________ when he was 17.
5. Nokia is very __________ in Europe and the Far East.
6. The Reebok __________ began in 1958.

Let's call it ...

They're all well-known companies, but where did they get their names from?

Bridgestone – The Japanese tyre company is named after its **founder**, Shojiro Ishibashi. His surname means stone bridge in Japanese.

Google – The name for the world's most **successful** search engine comes from the word *googol* – a huge number (1 followed by 100 noughts). It refers to the huge amount of information on the Internet.

Hyundai – The car **firm's** name means modern or fashionable in Korean.

Ikea – Work this one out. The Swedish furniture **business** was founded by Ingvar Kamprad. His family home was a farm called Elmtaryd, near the Swedish village of Agunnyard.

Nokia – Named after a small town in Finland that was home to a paper company. They later **produced** rubber **goods** and then had the idea of making mobile phones.

Reebok – The sports goods firm gets its name from the South African spelling of the word Rhebok, a type of fast-running African antelope.

Speaking

1 Work in groups. You all work for the same company and you want to produce a new and unique product. Turn to page 96 and follow the instructions.

CD-ROM For more activities go to **Choices Unit 2**

CHOICES

3 Outdoor life

LEARNING AIMS

- Can talk about future plans
- Can talk about the weather
- Can conduct simple interviews

Lead-in

1 Match the phrases in columns A and B to make folk sayings about the weather. Use the sound of the **bold** words to help you.

A	B
Rain before **seven**,	put on your hat or you'll wet your **head**.
Evening red and morning **grey**	before a **storm**.
Evening grey and morning **red**	fine weather is coming **soon**.
Red sky at **night**	are sure signs of a fine **day**.
When spiders weave their webs by **noon**	shepherds' **delight**.
Flies will **swarm**	fine before **eleven**.

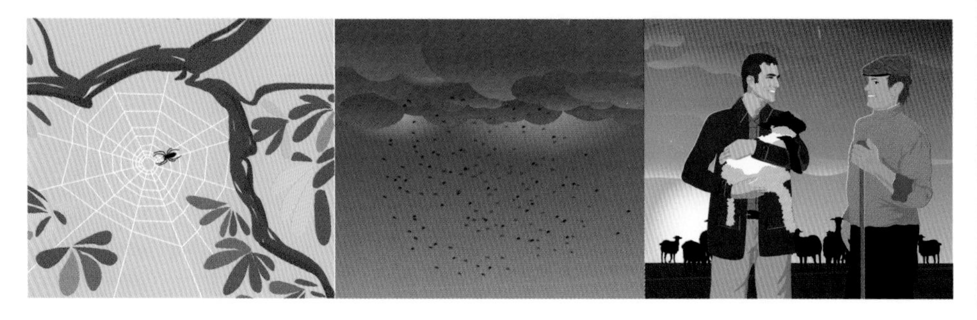

2 **07** Listen and check your answers.

3 Do you have any similar sayings in your country?

Working with the weather

Reading

1 Look at the title of the article on page 75. What does a weatherman do?

2 **08** Read the interview with Gary and match the interviewer's questions to Gary's answers.

3 Read the text again and complete these sentences.

1 Gary became a weatherman …
   a) because he wanted to be famous. b) by accident.
   c) because he wanted to work on television.

2 He likes his job because …
   a) old ladies love him. b) he travels a lot. c) it's interesting.

3 Gary's weather forecasts …
   a) are written by other people.
   b) use information from many different sources.
   c) are on the internet.

4 Gary …
   a) likes the producer of his weather programme.
   b) works on his own in the studio.
   c) works with a lot of other people.

5 This month Gary is working …
   a) until 3.00 am. b) on morning programmes.
   c) on afternoon and evening programmes.

6 Gary felt embarrassed because he …
   a) missed the football match. b) couldn't use the tickets.
   c) got the weather forecast wrong.

FAIR WEATHER MAN

 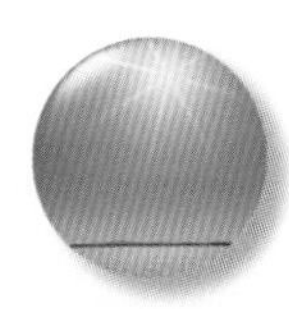    

Meet Gary Yates, meteorologist

How do you put together a weather forecast?
How did you become a weatherman?
Do you enjoy it?
What's it like in the studio?
Have you had any embarrassing moments doing the job?
When are your programmes on air?

1 ________________

Well, I was always interested in the weather as a child because I played football. We had a match every Saturday and I always watched the forecast on TV on Friday evenings. After I finished at university, I worked for a local radio station. One day in mid-December I was in Scotland. There was a terrible woman doing the weather – she couldn't read the names of the towns. The radio producer asked me to read the forecast. I did it for a week and I liked it. It was like doing a new puzzle every day. Then I went to night school and did a degree in meteorology.

2 ________________

Yes, I'm working for a satellite TV channel at the moment. I love being on TV. I feel much younger than I am and I love being a little bit famous. People recognise me from the TV – when I'm eating out at restaurants, when I'm filling the car at the petrol station and when I'm shopping. I have to say, though, that most of my fans are old ladies! Seriously though, I like my job because every day is different!

3 ________________

Some people think a weatherman just goes to the studio, stands in front of the camera and reads the weather. That's the easy part of the job. Most of the time I spend writing the forecast. I use a lot of different information – from satellite pictures, the Internet and so on. My job is to put all the information together and get the general picture. Then I make a good story out of it. I think it's important for a weather forecast to be like a story.

4 ________________

It's not like people think. There aren't any cameramen or engineers. Actually there's nobody else in the studio. When I go in, I put on the lights, turn on the microphone, and press a button that controls the cameras. When I go on air, I click through the charts and tell my story.

5 ________________

It depends. This month I'm doing the afternoon and evening forecasts at 5.00 pm, 5.30 pm, 10.00 pm and 11.00 pm. I start work at 3.45 pm and leave the studio at 11.45 pm. Next month I'm working on the morning shows. I think my wife prefers the late schedule. I don't go to bed until about three in the morning – and because I snore* she's quite happy!

6 ________________

Oh yes! One day I got a letter with two tickets for an important football match. At first I was really happy. I love football. But then I saw that the tickets were for the previous weekend. I read the letter and it said, 'You predicted rain and storms, so we didn't go to the match; but the weather was fantastic!' I felt terrible for a long time after that!

Glossary

* snore = to make a noise through your nose when you are sleeping

LANGUAGE STUDY

Present tenses and future plans

1 Match the sentences (a–d) to the uses (1–4).

a *When I go into the studio, I put on the lights and turn on the microphone.*
b *I love football.*
c *I'm working for a late night channel at the moment.*
d *Next month I'm working on the morning shows.*

1 Things you do every day.
2 A definite future plan.
3 True in general.
4 True for a period of time around now.

2 What tenses are the verbs in sentences a–d?

3 Complete these rules with *present simple* or *present continuous*. We use the:

1 ________________ to talk about routines and habits.
2 ________________ to talk about things happening now or in this period of time.
3 ________________ to talk about things which are generally true.
4 ________________ to talk about definite future plans, usually with a future time reference.

4 Complete these lists. Write the words and phrases with the tense we usually use them with.

~~always~~ ~~at the moment~~ every day every year never next year normally now sometimes this week today tomorrow usually

Present simple	**Present continuous**
always	*at the moment*
________	________

Grammar reference page 91

5 Complete the article with the present simple or present continuous form of the verbs.

Chus Lago (1 live) ________ in Spain. She (2 spend) ________ most of the year with her husband Antonio. Every year she (3 take) ________ a month off work to go exploring. This month Chus (4 walk) ________ across the North Pole. Unfortunately the weather has been too warm. The ice (5 melt) ________, and her radio (6 not work) ________ well. Because of this, a helicopter (7 coming) ________ to pick her up on 29th May. After that, Chus (8 fly) ________ back to Spain. She (9 arrive) ________ home on 1st June.

6 Write the questions for an interview with Chus Lago.

1 Where / live? — I live in the north of Spain.
2 What / do? — I'm an aerobics teacher.
3 What / do / now? — I'm walking in the Arctic.
4 travel / on your own? — No, I'm not. I'm travelling with a friend.
5 When / come / home? — Next week.

Speaking

1 Work with a partner. You are going to prepare an interview with an explorer.

1 Decide who is the journalist, and who is the explorer.
2 Use the questions in Language study Ex 6 to help you prepare questions.
3 Think of new answers for the explorer. Think about where he / she is from, what he / she is doing, and what his / her plans are.

2 Practise your interview and present it to the class.

What's the weather like?

Vocabulary and listening

1 Look at the weather words and describe the weather in the pictures.

It's cloudy
It's foggy
It's sunny
It's windy
It's stormy
It's raining
It's snowing
It's hot
It's warm
It's cold

2 Work with a partner. What do you like doing in different weather conditions? Find two things you have in common.

Example:
A: *I love sitting on a balcony when it's raining. I like listening to the rain on the trees outside.*
B: *I don't. I stay inside when it's raining. I don't like getting wet.*

3 **09** Listen to some extracts from commentaries at sporting events. What's the weather like at the different venues? Listen and complete the weather words on the website.

4 Which sports are popular in your country? When do people play them?

Speaking

1 Choose one of the sporting events in Vocabulary and listening Ex 3, or choose your own. You are planning to go to the event next weekend. Make notes. Think about where the event is, what your travel plans are, things to take with you and who you are going with.

2 Work in small groups. Ask and answer questions to find out about the events the other people in your group are going to.

3 In your group you have decided to go away together next weekend. Choose one of the events. Use the phrases in the box to help you.

What shall we do? I think Alex's idea's a good one. Let's go to ... Why don't we ...? I'd prefer not to ... because ...

CD-ROM For more activities go to **Choices Unit 3**

CHOICES

4 Advances

LEARNING AIMS

- Can express future intentions
- Can talk about modern inventions
- Can identify the main ideas in a radio programme

Inventions

Invention: cars

Advantages
- *They're fast*
- ___

Disadvantages
- *They're noisy*
- ___

Lead-in

1 What are these inventions? Choose one and note down some of its advantages and disadvantages.

2 Work with a partner who chose the same invention. Compare your ideas.

Listening

1 You are going to listen to part of a radio programme about inventions. Read the programme summaries from the radio website.

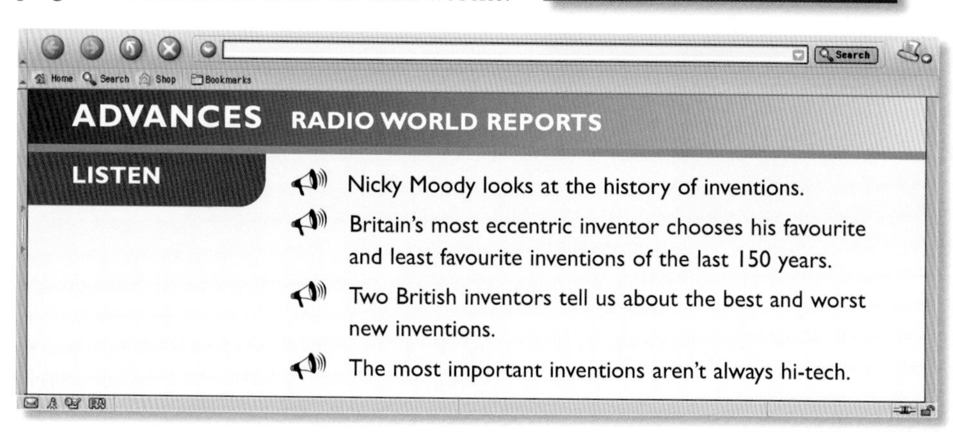

2 10 Which programme are you listening to?

3 Listen again. Are these statements true (T) or false (F)?

1. Tony's favourite invention is the CD. ☐
2. He's got 100 hours of music on his iPod. ☐
3. Annette's favourite invention is the TV remote control. ☐
4. Her husband watches a lot of sport on TV.
5. Listeners can vote for their favourite and least favourite inventions by phone. ☐

4 Do you agree with Tony and Annette's choices?

Vocabulary and pronunciation

1 These are some of the listeners' suggestions for their favourite and least favourite recent inventions. Match the words to the pictures.

camera phone	electric toothbrush	email	fake tan	GPS device
hairdryer	microwave food	non-alcoholic beer		

2 How often do you use these inventions? Write them on the line in the correct place for you.

3 Which two items are most important to you? Find someone else in the class with the same ideas.

4 11 Listen to the underlined vowel sounds in the words. (Circle) the word in each group with a different vowel sound.

1 /eə/ hairdryer where (email) compare
2 /aɪ/ device favourite hi-tech iPod
3 /əʊ/ phone remote world control
4 /eɪ/ email same fake camera
5 /aʊ/ microwave power hour about
6 /ɔɪ/ choices noisy television boy
7 /ɪə/ year nuclear beer idea

Speaking

1 Use one of the inventions on this page, or your own idea, and write your least favourite invention in the table.

Name	Least favourite invention	Why?
Susana	Electric toothbrush	They're expensive and silly. It's easier to use a normal toothbrush.

2 Complete the notes for your answer in the 'Why?' column of the table. Use the ideas in the box to help you.

> They're expensive / hard to use. It doesn't look / taste good.
> They don't work well. I don't have enough time ... There are too many ...
> It's easier / faster to ...

3 Work in groups and discuss your ideas. Which is the least favourite invention in your group? Compare your ideas with other groups.

Into the future

Reading and writing

1 Do you ever visit chat forums on the Internet? Do you think they are a good or bad idea? Why?

2 12 Read the chat forum thread. Which of these questions started the thread?

- What are you going to do after university?
- What kind of cars do you like?
- Would you like to be rich and famous?

3 Read the thread again and answer the questions.

1. What do you think of *sunwatcher's* idea?
2. Which people in the forum don't take *sunwatcher's* idea seriously?
3. Why does *Billben* want to see the designs for the engine?
4. What does *greencactus* think about the petrol companies?
5. What do you think of *mikethehawk's* suggestion?

4 Imagine you are *sunwatcher*. Write a reply to some of the entries.

5 Work in a group. Read each others' replies. Which do you like best?

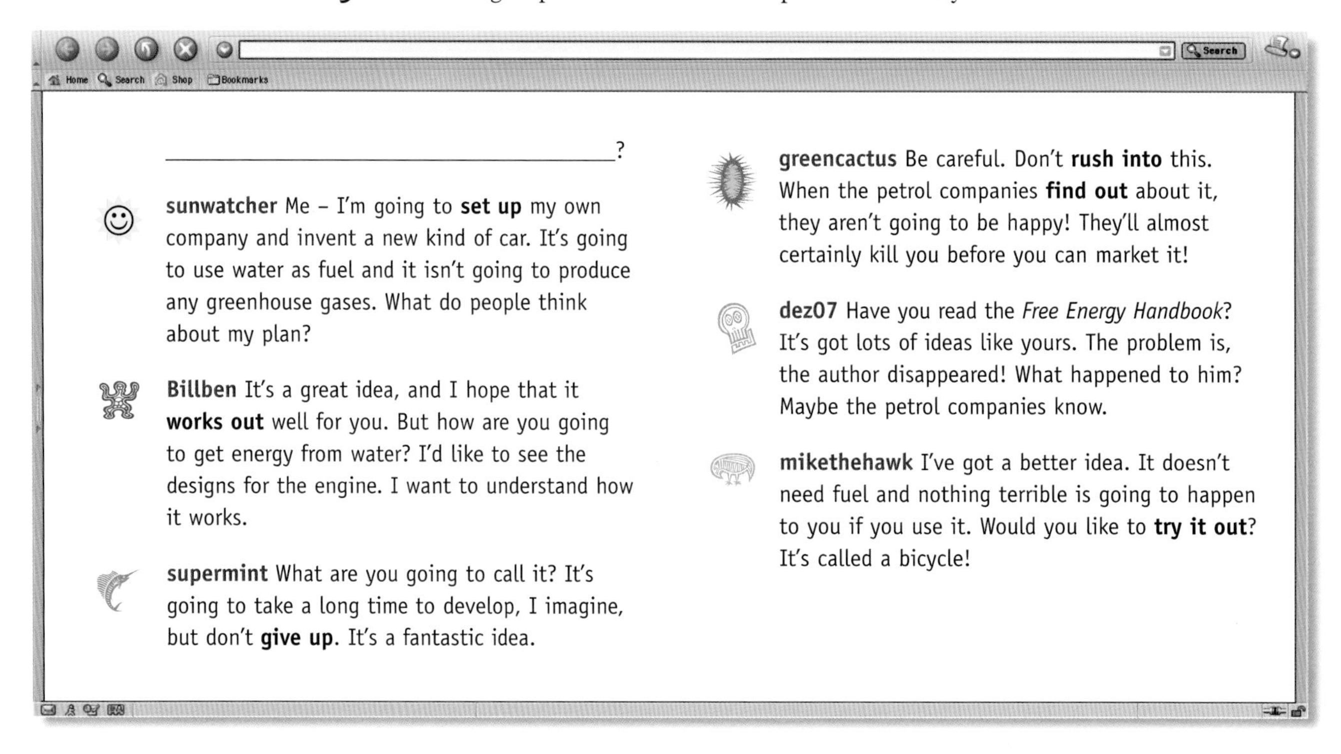

______________________________________?

sunwatcher Me – I'm going to **set up** my own company and invent a new kind of car. It's going to use water as fuel and it isn't going to produce any greenhouse gases. What do people think about my plan?

Billben It's a great idea, and I hope that it **works out** well for you. But how are you going to get energy from water? I'd like to see the designs for the engine. I want to understand how it works.

supermint What are you going to call it? It's going to take a long time to develop, I imagine, but don't **give up**. It's a fantastic idea.

greencactus Be careful. Don't **rush into** this. When the petrol companies **find out** about it, they aren't going to be happy! They'll almost certainly kill you before you can market it!

dez07 Have you read the *Free Energy Handbook*? It's got lots of ideas like yours. The problem is, the author disappeared! What happened to him? Maybe the petrol companies know.

mikethehawk I've got a better idea. It doesn't need fuel and nothing terrible is going to happen to you if you use it. Would you like to **try it out**? It's called a bicycle!

Vocabulary

1 Replace the underlined words in these sentences with the correct form of the phrasal verbs in **bold** in the text.

1. Sometimes an invention takes years to develop. But a good inventor never stops.
2. Marta discovered a lot about famous inventors on the Internet.
3. When Laila saw the exercise machine, she wanted to use it straight away.
4. Don't make a really quick decision about buying a new car. Choose carefully before you buy one.
5. I tried to invent and sell some new computer software, but it was unsuccessful. Very few people bought it.
6. I'm starting a new company with some friends.

2 Work with a partner and discuss these questions.

1. Have you ever rushed into something? What happened? Did it work out?
2. Do you enjoy trying out new things straight away, or do you prefer to wait?
3. Have you ever set up a business, or do you know someone who has? What sort of business was it?
4. Have you ever tried to give up something – like smoking? Were you successful?

LANGUAGE STUDY

Talking about the future

1 Look at these sentences and tick the correct box below.

*I'm **going to** invent a new kind of car.*
*It **isn't going to** produce any greenhouse gases.*
*What **are you going to** call your invention?*

We use the ***going to*** future to talk about ...

a definite plans ☐ b intentions ☐ *Grammar reference page 91*

2 What are these people going to do? Write sentences with the verbs in the box.

do	have	listen	play	watch	write

Example: *He's going to do the shopping.*

3 Work with a partner. Imagine you are one of the people in the pictures and talk about your intentions. Your partner must guess who you are. Continue in the same way with all the people.

Example:
I'm going to be very quick.
I'm not going to spend a lot of money.
I'm only going to buy a few things.

Class chat forum

Writing

1 Complete one of these questions for your classmates to start a chat forum thread. Write it at the top of a sheet of paper.

Who's going to ...? Are you going to ...? Is anyone going to ...?

2 Work in a group. Pass your question sheet to the person on your right. Read the new question. Write your entry and pass it on.

3 When you get back your original question sheet, read the thread. Which of the entries do you find the most interesting? Tell your group.

CD-ROM For more activities go to **Choices Unit 4**

CHOICES

5 Review

Lead-in

1 Write six sentences on a piece of paper, then give it to your teacher.

- Three exciting things you've done in your life.
- Three things that you've never done but you'd like to do.

I've ridden a camel. I haven't been surfing.

2 Your teacher will give you someone else's piece of paper. Ask questions to find out who it belongs to.

Example:
A: *Gerard, have you ever ridden a camel?*
B: *No, I haven't.*

Vocabulary

1 13 Listen to Hugh talking about some of his memories. Underline the things he talks about.

1. his first car / his father's first car
2. his first journey by train / his first journey by plane
3. the warm weather in Cornwall / the foggy weather in London
4. his first television / the first time he watched television

2 Listen again, then complete the gaps in the sentences.

1. My father's car had a __________ on the outside.
2. In my __________ we were all boys.
3. The journey was very long and __________.
4. In London it was always __________ or __________.
5. It was __________ for people to have televisions at home.

3 Put these words in the correct word groups.

boarding card camera cheap cloudy common computer GPS device easy gate hairdryer hot microwave old-fashioned passenger platform rainy stormy terminal unpopular warm

inventions	transport	weather adjectives	other adjectives
__________	__________	__________	__________
__________	__________	__________	__________
__________	__________	__________	__________
__________	__________	__________	__________
__________	__________	__________	__________

4 Which of these 'firsts' in your life do you remember? Make a list.

- The first time I saw a lot of snow.
- My first car or bike.
- The first time I travelled by plane.
- My first mobile phone.
- The first time I went on a long journey.
- The first time I wrote an email.
- The first DVD I bought.
- My first Mp3 player.
- The first time I used a computer.

5 Look at your partner's list. Ask your partner questions about the things he or she remembers.

Example:
How old were you when you first saw snow?

Language study

1 Read the questions on the 'Speaking bee' board. Make some notes about each of the topics.

2 Work in groups of four students. Read how to play 'Speaking bee' and play the game.

START 1 23 17 5 11 14 FINISH

START 13 8 12 15 7 20 FINISH

START 21 3 16 2 10 4 FINISH

START 18 9 19 6 22 24 FINISH

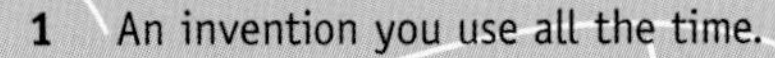

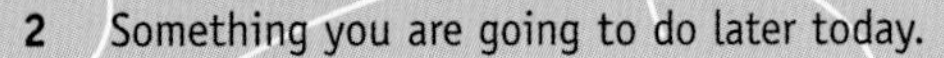

Speaking bee

How to play

Each group needs four counters and a watch with a second hand.

1. The youngest player starts. Move your counter one square – in the direction you choose. You must speak about the topic on the square for as long as possible.
2. If you speak without stopping or changing the subject for:
   less than 10 seconds: **1 point**
   between 10 and 20 seconds: **5 points**
   between 20 and 30 seconds: **10 points**
   more than 30 seconds: **15 points**
3. When the first person reaches FINISH, stop the game. This person gets 15 points.
4. The winner is the player with the highest number of points.

Tell us about ...

1 An invention you use all the time.
2 Something you are going to do later today.
3 The most important things you've done this year.
4 Your favourite and least favourite months of the year.
5 Your plans for this evening.
6 Interesting places you have visited.
7 The differences between two of your friends.
8 The best film you've ever seen.
9 Your weekend routine.
10 Your plans for next weekend.
11 The clothes you are wearing today.
12 Your favourite TV programme.
13 The last sports event you went to or took part in.
14 The places where you have lived.
15 Something you intend to do in the future.
16 The book you're reading at the moment.
17 The differences between two well-known cities.
18 The weather today.
19 Your plans for the next year.
20 Something that has worked out well for you.
21 Your earliest memory.
22 The differences between a car and a bike.
23 The worst invention of all time.
24 The longest journey you've been on.

Song

1 Read the factfile about *Supertramp*. Are these statements true (T) or false (F)?

1. The members of *Supertramp* played together at school.
2. Their first album was very successful.
3. They started playing different music after they became famous.
4. Their most successful album was *Breakfast in America*.

factfile

In 1969 a Dutch millionaire gave his friend, Rick Davies, a lot of money to start a band. Rick put an advert in a music magazine and *Supertramp* was born. The group made two unsuccessful albums and the millionaire didn't give them any more money.

Supertramp had no money and not many fans. They wanted to stay together and they needed a hit. They started playing a different kind of music. Their third album, *Crime of the century* was a hit and *Supertramp* became famous. In 1979 they had their biggest hit with the album *Breakfast in America*. It sold more than 18 million copies worldwide, and Supertramp became international superstars. The hit single *The logical song*, was on this album.

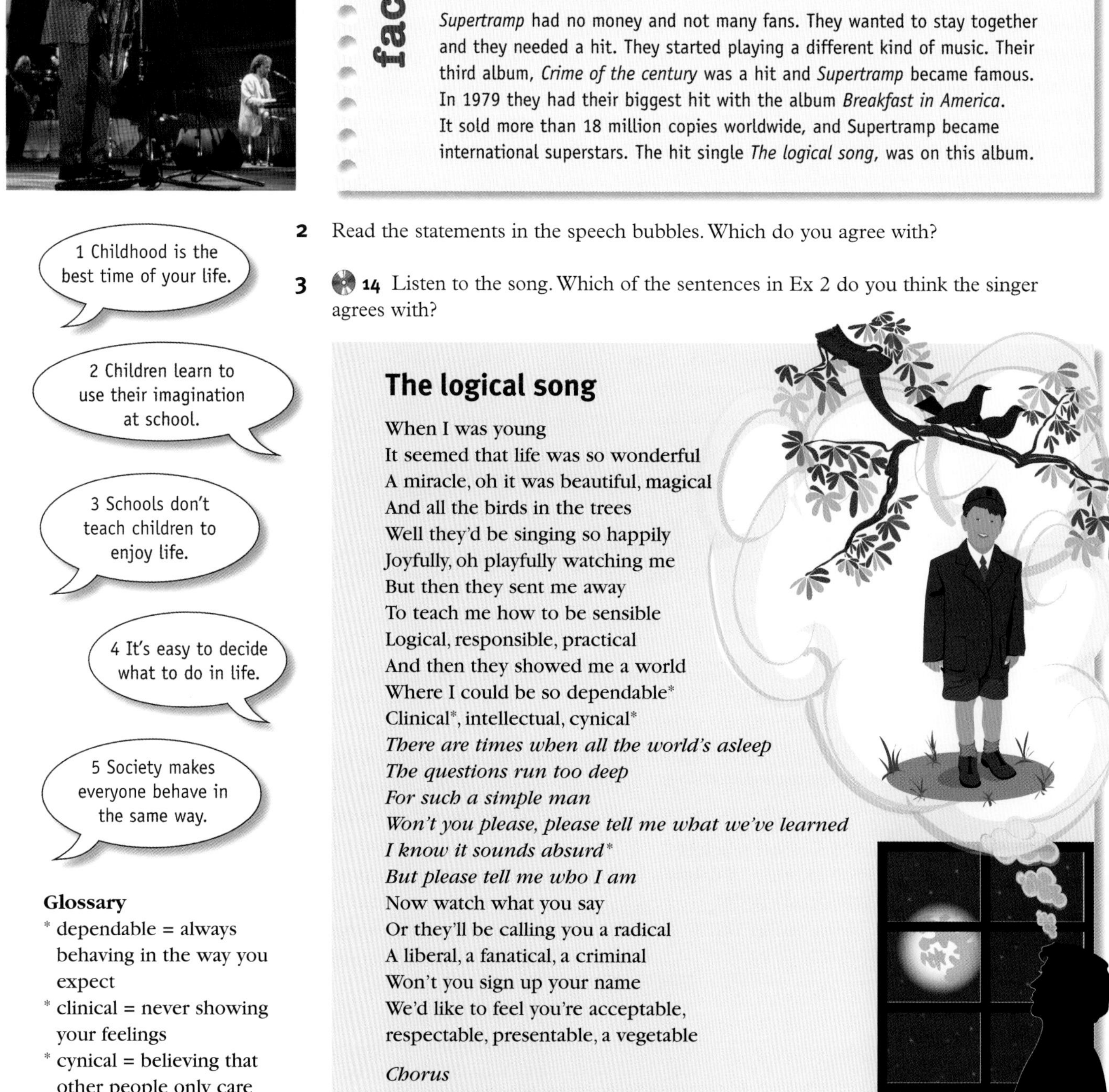

2 Read the statements in the speech bubbles. Which do you agree with?

1 Childhood is the best time of your life.

2 Children learn to use their imagination at school.

3 Schools don't teach children to enjoy life.

4 It's easy to decide what to do in life.

5 Society makes everyone behave in the same way.

3 14 Listen to the song. Which of the sentences in Ex 2 do you think the singer agrees with?

The logical song

When I was young
It seemed that life was so wonderful
A miracle, oh it was beautiful, magical
And all the birds in the trees
Well they'd be singing so happily
Joyfully, oh playfully watching me
But then they sent me away
To teach me how to be sensible
Logical, responsible, practical
And then they showed me a world
Where I could be so dependable*
Clinical*, intellectual, cynical*
There are times when all the world's asleep
The questions run too deep
For such a simple man
Won't you please, please tell me what we've learned
*I know it sounds absurd**
But please tell me who I am
Now watch what you say
Or they'll be calling you a radical
A liberal, a fanatical, a criminal
Won't you sign up your name
We'd like to feel you're acceptable,
respectable, presentable, a vegetable

Chorus
At night when all the world's asleep …
so logical … digital … so unbelievable

Glossary

* dependable = always behaving in the way you expect
* clinical = never showing your feelings
* cynical = believing that other people only care about themselves
* absurd = very funny or stupid

4 Listen again. Underline the words with this stress pattern. How many can you find?

O o o
Example: *sensible*

Speaking: you are what you buy ...

Step 1: Making choices

- Look at the products in the pictures. You want to buy one of each thing. Choose one that matches your lifestyle. Choose a product from each group and complete the table.

Product	Choice	Reason
car	*the smallest one*	*it's easier to park, it's cheaper, ...*
camera		
phone		
computer		
bed		

Step 2: Exchanging opinions

- Work with a partner. Talk about the things you are both going to buy. Note down your partner's choices.

Product	Choice	Reason
car		
camera		
phone		
computer		
bed		

Step 3: Analysing the results

- Look at your partner's choices. What do they tell you about his / her character? Look at the choices below. Which do you think is more important for your partner? Put a cross (✗) on each line to show your opinion.

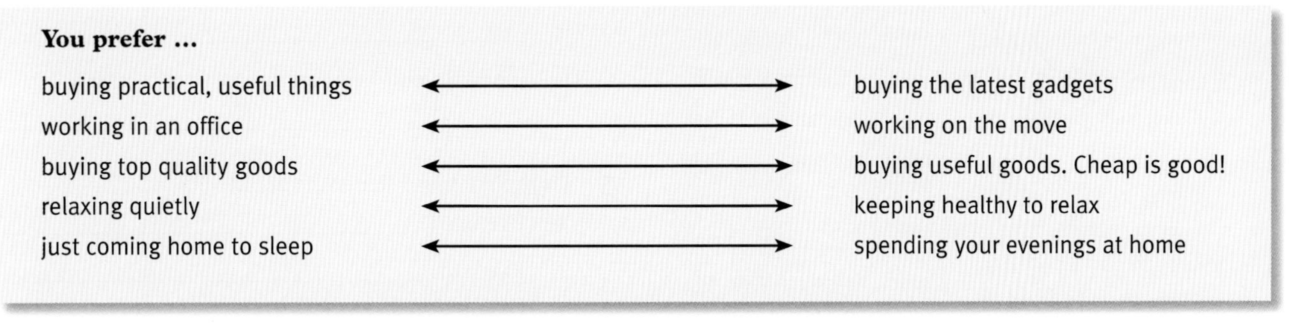

You prefer ...

buying practical, useful things	⟷	buying the latest gadgets
working in an office	⟷	working on the move
buying top quality goods	⟷	buying useful goods. Cheap is good!
relaxing quietly	⟷	keeping healthy to relax
just coming home to sleep	⟷	spending your evenings at home

- Tell your partner your guesses. Were you right?

Extra practice

Unit 1

1 Put the letters in the correct order to complete these sentences.

1 Sorry, no more *p*__________, the bus is full. S S A E N S G E R
2 Can you meet me at the *a*__________? T R P O I R
3 Could I see your *b*__________ *c*__________, please? D O A R I N G D A R
4 Get out your tickets. The *t*__________ *i*__________ is coming. C K T E I T R S P E C O N
5 Please go to *g*__________ number 15. T E A
6 Here comes the train! Which *c*__________ are we in? G I E A S A R R
7 The *t*__________ *o*__________ closes at midnight. E T I K C C F F I E
8 Your train leaves from *p*__________ 6 in ten minutes. O R F L A T M
9 Excuse me, is someone sitting in this *s*____? T E A

2 Complete the text with the past participle of the verbs in the box.

be buy do drink eat fly meet ride see swim take

I've (1)________ some really amazing things in my life. I've (2)________ across the Atlantic in a hot air balloon and I've (3)________ whales at the North Pole. I've (4)________ underwater with dolphins and I've (5)________ elephants in India. I've (6)________ Chinese food and I've (7)________ yak's milk in Tibet. I've (8)________ photos of princes and I've (9)________ the Queen of England. I've (10)________ souvenirs from all the countries I've visited too. But the best thing of all is that I've never (11)________ abroad. I'm a virtual traveller you see! I travel in my imagination on the Internet and through books!

3 Jill is an explorer. Write sentences about her life using the present perfect.

Example:
visit / many different countries
Jill has visited many different countries.

1 climb / Mount Everest / without oxygen
____
2 write / a book about her travels
____
3 meet / a lot of interesting people
____
4 go / North Pole
____
5 send / email messages / from Antarctica
____
6 never / be / married
____

4 Are the verbs in these sentences correct (✓) or incorrect (✗)? Correct the sentences with mistakes.

Example:
Last week Melike has been to Vienna. ✗
Last week Melike went to Vienna.

1 My mother has been to China.
____
2 Jim has travelled to Poland last year.
____
3 We have never studied French.
____
4 When have you bought that book?
____
5 Did you buy anything on Saturday?
____
6 They haven't been on holiday last month.
____

5 Complete these sentences about you.

1 I've lived ______________________________
2 I've had ______________________________
3 I've never been ______________________________
4 I've met ______________________________
5 I've never flown ______________________________
6 I've never done ______________________________

Unit 2

1 Write the opposites of the adjectives in the word puzzle.

1 fashionable
2 horrible
3 slow
4 uncomfortable
5 cheap
6 unusual
7 unpopular
8 unknown
9 heavy

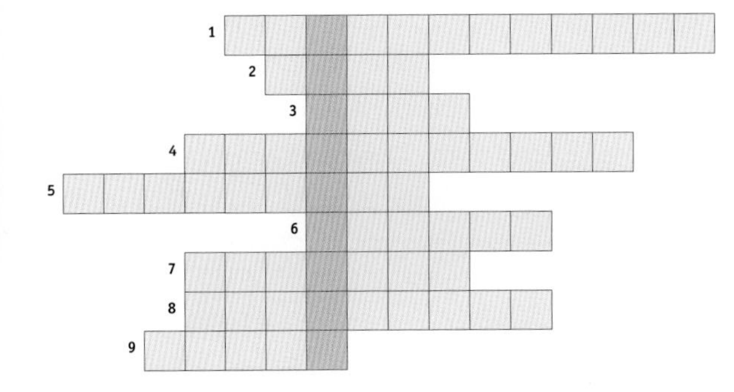

2 Write the hidden adjective: _ _ _ _ _ _ _ _ _ _ and its opposite: _ _ _ _

3 Use the rules from page 72 to write the comparative and the superlative forms of the adjectives.

Adjective	Comparative	Superlative
angry	*angrier*	*the angriest*
boring		
easy		
happy		
interesting		
late		
long		
relaxing		
sad		
small		
warm		

4 Complete the questions with superlative forms. Then choose the correct answer.

1 Which is (successful) ___________ pop album ever?
a) *Thriller*, Michael Jackson
b) *Escapology*, Robbie Williams
c) *Come on over*, Shania Twain

2 Which is (busy) ___________ international airport in the world?
a) Charles de Gaulle, Paris
b) John F. Kennedy, New York
c) Heathrow, London

3 How tall was (tall) ___________ man ever?
a) 2.22 metres b) 2.72 metres c) 3.02 metres

4 How many computers are there in the world's (big) ___________ Cyber Café.
a) 1,000 b) 150 c) 760

5 Which is (popular) ___________ internet search engine in the world?
a) Google b) Yahoo c) Searchalot

6 Which is (expensive) ___________ place to rent an office?
a) New York b) London c) Paris

Answers

1a 2c 3b 4c 5a 6b

5 Write a comparative and a superlative sentence comparing each group of products.

1 a bicycle a Harley Davidson a scooter

____

____

2 a Rolls Royce a Ferrari a Smart car

____

____

3 a discman a walkman an MP3 player

____

____

4 a hamburger a salad a bag of crisps

____

____

Unit 3

1 Look at the weather forecast and complete the sentences about the cities.

Around the world

Weather	°C	°F		
Algiers	20	68	cld	rn
Budapest	9	48	fg	fg
Buenos Aires	31	87	s	s
Cairo	18	64	rn	cld
Moscow	-14	6	sn	sn
Singapore	31	88	st	bw
Vancouver	7	45	wd	wd

1 In Buenos Aires it's _ _ _ and _ _ _ _ _.
2 In Algiers it's _ _ _ _ _ _ _ _ but _ _ _ _.
3 In Budapest it's _ _ _ _ and _ _ _ _ _
4 It's _ _ _ _ _ _ today in Cairo but it isn't _ _ _ _.
5 In Singapore it's _ _ _ and _ _ _ _ _ _ with rain forecast all day.
6 It's _ _ _ _ _ _ _ _ today in Moscow.
7 In Vancouver today it's very _ _ _ _ _.

2 Complete the dialogue with the present simple or present continuous form of the verbs.

M: Hi Ben.
B: Oh, hi Mum. How are you?

M: Great. We (1 have) __________ a fantastic time here in Istanbul.
B: What's the weather like?
M: It's quite warm, but it (2 get) __________ cold in the evenings.
B: And what are the people like?
M: They're very friendly – and lots of people (3 speak) __________ English. So that's OK.
B: How's Dad?
M: He's fine. He (4 watch) __________ a football match right now. And what (5 do) __________?
B: I (6 send) __________ some emails. Frank and I (7 play) __________ tennis later this evening.
M: How are Lily and Rose?
B: They're fine. Rose (8 stay) __________ at Ana's house tonight and Lily (9 wait) __________ for Dan. They (10 go) __________ to the cinema tonight.
M: Well, give them all my love. And see you on Saturday.
B: On Saturday? (11 not / come) __________ back on Sunday?
M: No, we (12 get) __________ the plane on Saturday morning. Why?
B: Well ... it's just that I (13 use) __________ the car to take Kate to the coast on Saturday, so I can't pick you up from the airport.
A: Oh!

3 Tick (✓) the correct sentence in each pair.

1 a Why are you wearing a jacket? It's hot today. ☐
  b I'm usually wearing a dress when I go out. ☐
2 a Tim doesn't like football but he loves motorbike racing. ☐
  b 'Where's Tim?' 'He rides his motorbike.' ☐
3 a We do an English exam tomorrow. ☐
  b We have classes every day of the week for two hours. ☐
4 a How often do you play tennis? ☐
  b Are you playing tennis every Saturday? ☐
5 a The horses aren't racing here today because of heavy rain. ☐
  b The horses aren't racing when the weather is bad. ☐

4 Write as many true sentences as you can about yourself using the words below.

At the moment This week Today Tomorrow Next month This year	and but	nearly always usually normally sometimes hardly ever

Examples:
At the moment I'm writing in English, but I usually write in Polish.
This year I'm going on holiday to Canada, but I hardly ever go on holiday.

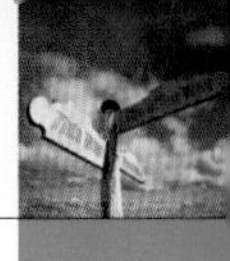

Unit 4

1 Use the clues to complete the crossword with recent inventions.

Across

2 Many people think that playing this is bad for you.
6 It's great if your skin is a very light colour.
7 You use this to find websites.
9 You use these to write to people without using a pen and paper.
10 Programs for computers.
11 An ___ toothbrush has power.

Down

1 You use it to take photos.
3 You usually use this first thing in the morning and late at night.
4 It's quick and easy but not very healthy.
5 You use it to dry your hair.
8 This GPS ___ is useful if you often get lost.

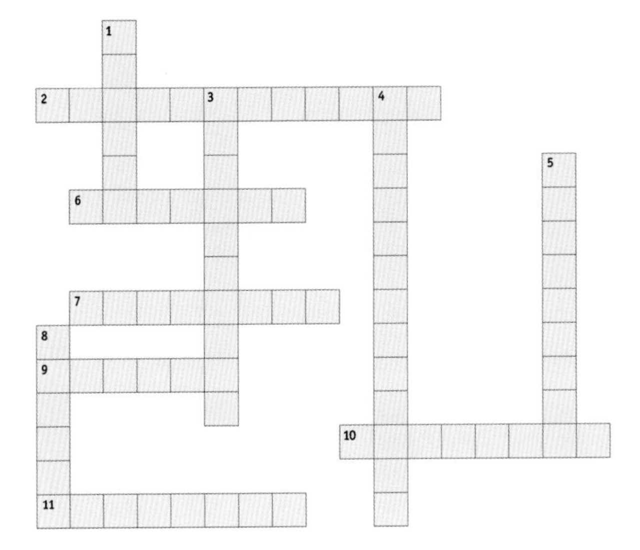

2 What jobs are they going to do? Complete the sentences with your ideas.

Example:
Tom likes making new things.
He's going to be an inventor.

1 Ahmet loves flying.
_______________ a flight attendant.
2 Julia is studying medicine at university.
_______________ a doctor.
3 Jack and Ryan play football very well.
_______________ footballers.
4 We like writing.
_______________ journalists.
5 I want to be famous.
_______________ a film star.
6 You are very good with children.
_______________ a teacher.

3 Bridget had a terrible day yesterday. Read about her day then write her intentions for tomorrow in her diary.

1 She went to a party the previous evening.
2 She got up late and missed her bus to work.
3 She's on a diet but she had a hamburger and chips for lunch.
4 She fell asleep at work and her manager got angry with her.
5 She went shopping with her best friend Linda and spent all her money.
6 She left her laptop computer on the bus and couldn't get her messages.
7 She watched TV all evening with her flatmates.

1 *I'm not going to go out tomorrow evening.*
____
2 _______________
____
3 _______________
____
4 _______________
____
5 _______________
____
6 _______________
____
7 _______________
____

4 Which of your habits do you want to change? Write about your good intentions for the next month.

Grammar reference

Unit 1

Present perfect simple

Positive and negative

	have	past participle	
I You We They	have haven't 've never	been seen travelled	to Egypt. the Pyramids. by boat.
He She It	has hasn't 's never		

Questions

Have I / you / we / they ever been to Egypt?
Has he / she / it ever been to Egypt?

Regular and irregular past participles

The past participle of regular verbs is the same as the past simple form.

Some of the most common verbs in English have irregular past participles.

Infinitives and past participles

be → *been*	*go* → *gone*
buy → *bought*	*have* → *had*
come → *come*	*meet* → *met*
do → *done*	*read* → *read*
drink → *drank*	*ride* → *ridden*
drive → *driven*	*send* → *sent*
eat → *eaten*	*swim* → *swum*
fly → *flown*	*taken* → *taken*
get → *got*	*write* → *written*

Use

You can use the present perfect simple to talk about an activity or activities that happened at some time in the past. This is the **life experience** use of the present perfect simple.
*He'**s travelled** all over the world.*
*They'**ve** never **been** interested in travelling.*
***Have** you ever **seen** an elephant?*

You don't say **when** the activity happened.
She's been to New York twice in her life. (You don't know exactly when.)

have / *has been* can be the present perfect form of *be*
– *They'**ve** never **been** interested.*
or *go* (and *come back*)
– *She'**s been** to New York twice.*

You use the past simple to say when something happened.
He went to Istanbul last year. (You know when it happened.)

***ever* / *never* and the present perfect simple**
You use *ever* in questions or negative sentences to mean 'in that person's life'.
You use *never* in sentences to mean 'at no time'.

Unit 2

Comparing things

The comparative and superlative forms of adjectives depend on the number of syllables each adjective has.

Most adjectives with one syllable:
add *-er* / *-est*

Adjective	Comparative	Superlative
cheap	cheap**er**	the cheap**est**
fast	fast**er**	the fast**est**
slow	slow**er**	the slow**est**
weak	weak**er**	the weak**est**

One syllable adjectives that end in *-e:*
add *-r* / *-st*

Adjective	Comparative	Superlative
large	large**r**	the large**st**
nice	nice**r**	the nice**st**

One syllable adjectives that end in consonant + vowel + consonant:
double the final consonant + *-er* / *-est*

Adjective	Comparative	Superlative
big	big**ger**	the big**gest**
fat	fat**ter**	the fat**test**
hot	hot**ter**	the hot**test**
wet	wet**ter**	the wet**test**

Adjectives with two syllables that end in *-y:*
change *-y* to *-ier* / *-iest*

Adjective	Comparative	Superlative
angry	angr**ier**	the angr**iest**
busy	bus**ier**	the bus**iest**
easy	eas**ier**	the eas**iest**
healthy	health**ier**	the health**iest**
heavy	heav**ier**	the heav**iest**
ugly	ugl**ier**	the ugl**iest**

Other adjectives with two or more syllables
add *more* / *the most*:

Adjective	Comparative	Superlative
useful	**more** useful	**the most** useful
attractive	**more** attractive	**the most** attractive
comfortable	**more** comfortable	**the most** comfortable
expensive	**more** expensive	**the most** expensive
fashionable	**more** fashionable	**the most** fashionable
popular	**more** popular	**the most** popular
unusual	**more** unusual	**the most** unusual

Irregular forms

Adjective	Comparative	Superlative
bad	worse	the worst
far	further	the furthest
good	better	the best

Use

You use **comparatives** when you want to compare two things. In these sentences you use comparative adjective + *than* + noun / pronoun:
The Superzoom is more expensive than the Snapshot.
This camera is bigger than that one.

You use **object pronouns** after comparative + *than*:
Jane is healthier than ***me****.*
I'm taller than ***her****.*

You use **superlatives** to talk about the difference between one thing and the others in a group.
It's ***the best*** *book* [of all the books] *I've ever read.*
Mount Everest is ***the highest*** *mountain* [of all the mountains] *in the world.*
Maria is ***the most intelligent*** *student* [of all the students] *in the class.*

Unit 3

Ways of talking about present times

Turn to pages 26–27 for notes on the present simple.
Turn to page 27 for notes on the present continuous.

There are lots of ways of talking about present time.

You use the **present simple** to talk about routines and habits and to express things that are true in general.
I ***play*** *tennis on Thursdays.* (routine)
He ***drinks*** *coffee at breakfast.* (habit)
*It****'s*** *often foggy in Manchester.* (generally true)

You often use time references like these with the present simple to help explain the details of the routines, habits or general truths.
Examples: *always, every day, every year, never, normally, often, sometimes, usually.*

You use the **present continuous** to describe activities that are happening now or in this period of time.
I'm watching *a football match at the moment.*
I'm living *in London this month, but I usually live in York.*

With the present continuous for activities now, or around now, you often use time references:
Examples: *at the moment, now, this month, this week, today.*

Future plans

You can use the present continuous to talk about definite future plans. You usually use it with a specific future time reference.
Examples: *at 8 o'clock, on Friday, tomorrow, next year, next month.*

Tomorrow I'm starting work at 8 o'clock.
Are you coming to the party on Friday?
Chus isn't going to the North Pole next year.

Unit 4

Talking about the future: *going to*

Positive and negative

	be	+ *going to*	+ infinitive
I	'm (am) 'm not	going to	invent a new energy drink.
You We They	're (are) aren't		
He She It	's (is) isn't isn't		

Questions

Are	you we they	going to set up a new business?
Is	he she it	

Use

You use the *going to* future to talk about intentions.
One day I'm ***going to*** *be an inventor.*
They aren't ***going to*** *do the exam.*
When is she ***going to*** *get married?*

With the verb *go* you often use the present continuous form for future intentions and plans instead of *going to*.
Are *you* ***going*** *to the cinema this evening?* (not *going to go*)
*We****'re going*** *on holiday to Turkey in the summer.*
He ***isn't going*** *shopping this afternoon.*

CHOICES

Wordlist

*** the 2,500 most common English words, ** very common words, * fairly common words

Unit 1

Argentina *n* /ˌɑ:dʒən'ti:nə/
bagel *n* /'beɪgl/
bazaar *n* /bə'zɑ:/
boarding card *n* /'bɔ:dɪŋ ˌkɑ:d/
book *v* /bʊk/ **
bus *n* /bʌs/ ***
bus driver *n* /'bʌs ˌdraɪvə/
bus stop *n* /'bʌs ˌstɒp/
camel *n* /'kæml/
carriage *n* /'kærɪdʒ/ *
check-in *n* /'tʃek ɪn/
China *n* /'tʃaɪnə/
departure board *n* /dɪ'pɑ:tʃə ˌbɔ:d/
destination *n* /ˌdestɪ'neɪʃn/ **
Egypt *n* /'i:dʒɪpt/
Excuse me *phrase* /ɪk'skju:z ˌmi:/
find *v* /faɪnd/ ***
flight *n* /flaɪt/ ***
gate *n* /geɪt/ ***
incredible *adj* /ɪn'kredəbl/ *
location *n* /ləʊ'keɪʃn/ ***
on time *phrase* /ˌɒn 'taɪm/
passenger *n* /'pæsɪndʒə/ ***
people *n* /'pi:pl/ ***
plane *n* /pleɪn/ ***
platform *n* /'plætˌfɔ:m/ **
postcard *n* /'pəʊstˌkɑ:d/ *
prize *n* /praɪz/ ***
railway station *n* /'reɪlweɪ ˌsteɪʃn/
relaxing *adj* /rɪ'læksɪŋ/
seat *n* /si:t/ ***
shopping *n* /'ʃɒpɪŋ/ **
sightseeing *n* /'saɪtˌsi:ɪŋ/
single ticket *n* /'sɪŋgl ˌtɪkɪt/
souvenir *n* /ˌsu:və'nɪə/ *
spa *n* /spɑ:/
surf *v* /sɜ:f/ *
sushi *n* /'su:ʃi/
take photos *phrase* /ˌteɪk 'fəʊtəʊz/
terminal *n* /'tɜ:mɪnəl/ **
Thailand *n* /'taɪlænd/
thing *n* /θɪŋ/ ***
ticket *n* /'tɪkɪt/ ***
ticket inspector *n* /'tɪkɪt ɪnˌspektə/
ticket office *n* /'tɪkɪt ˌɒfɪs/
tour *n, v* /tʊə/ ***
train *n* /treɪn/ ***
Turkey *n* /'tɜ:ki/
UAE *n* /ˌju: eɪ 'i:/
unusual *adj* /ʌn'ju:ʒʊəl/ ***
visit *v* /'vɪzɪt/ ***
voucher *n* /'vaʊtʃə/

Unit 2

advert *n* /'ædvɜ:t/ *
advertise *v* /'ædvətaɪz/ **
aftershave *n* /'ɑ:ftəˌʃeɪv/
antelope *n* /'æntɪˌləʊp/
beauty *n* /'bju:ti/ ***
brand *n* /brænd/ **
bridge *n* /brɪdʒ/ ***
business *n* /'bɪznəs/ ***
car *n* /kɑ:/ ***
cheap *adj* /tʃi:p/ ***
chewing gum *n* /'tʃu:ɪŋ ˌgʌm/
climbing boot *n* /'klaɪmɪŋ ˌbu:t/
comfortable *adj* /'kʌmftəbl/ ***
common *adj* /'kɒmən/ ***
computer game *n* /kəm'pju:tə ˌgeɪm/
difficult *adj* /'dɪfɪklt/ ***
digital camera *n* /ˌdɪdʒɪtl 'kæmərə/
dog food *n* /'dɒg ˌfu:d/
easy *adj* /'i:zi/ ***
exercise *v* /'eksəˌsaɪz/ ***
expensive *adj* /ɪk'spensɪv/ ***
fashionable *adj* /'fæʃnəbl/ **
fast *adj* /fɑ:st/ ***
firm *n* /fɜ:m/ ***
fizzy *adj* /'fɪzi/
found *v* /faʊnd/ ***
founder *n* /'faʊndə/ *
furniture *n* /'fɜ:nɪtʃə/ ***
glasses *n* /'glɑ:sɪz/ *
goods *n* /gʊdz/ ***
googol *n* /'gu:gɒl/
health *n* /helθ/ ***
horrible *adj* /'hɒrəbl/ **
lemonade *n* /ˌlemə'neɪd/
light *adj* /laɪt/ ***
magazine *n* /ˌmægə'zi:n/ ***
mineral *n* /'mɪnərəl/ *
modern *adj* /'mɒdən/ ***
muscle *n* /'mʌsl/ ***
nice *adj* /naɪs/ ***
old-fashioned *adj* /ˌəʊld 'fæʃnd/ **
paper *n* /'peɪpə/ ***
perfume *n* /'pɜ:fju:m/ *
piano *n* /pi'ænəʊ/ **
pill *n* /pɪl/ *
popular *adj* /'pɒpjʊlə/ ***
price *n* /praɪs/ ***
produce *v* /prə'dju:s/ ***
pyjamas *n* /pə'dʒɑ:məz/ *
recommend *v* /ˌrekə'mend/ ***
search engine *n* /'sɜ:tʃ ˌendʒɪn/**
slow *adj* /sləʊ/ ***
stone *n* /stəʊn/ ***
successful *adj* /sək'sesfl/ ***
tyre *n* /'taɪə/ **
uncomfortable *adj* /ʌn'kʌmftəbl/ **
unknown *adj* /ʌn'nəʊn/ **
unpopular *adj* /ʌn'pɒpjʊlə/ *
vitamin *n* /'vɪtəmɪn/ **
washing powder *n* /'wɒʃɪŋ ˌpaʊdə/
watch *n* /wɒtʃ/ **
well-known *adj* /ˌwel (nəʊn/ **

Unit 3

afternoon *n* /ˌɑ:ftə'nu:n/ ***
become *v* /bɪ'kʌm/ ***
button *n* /'bʌtn/ ***
chart *n* /tʃɑ:t/ **
cloudy *adj* /'klaʊdi/
cold *adj* /kəʊld/ ***
control *v* /kən'trəʊl/ ***
depend *v* /dɪ'pend/ ***
embarrassed *adj* /ɪm'bærəst/ *
embarrassing *adj* /ɪm'bærəsɪŋ/ *
evening *n* /'i:vnɪŋ/ ***
fan *n* /fæn/ **
fine *adj* /faɪn/ ***
foggy *adj* /'fɒgi/
forecast *n* /'fɔ:kɑ:st/ **
general *adj* /'dʒenərəl/ ***
hot *adj* /hɒt/ ***
ice *n* /aɪs/ ***
information *n* /ˌɪnfə'meɪʃn/ ***
light *n* /laɪt/ ***
match *n* /mætʃ/ ***
melt *v* /melt/ **
meteorologist *n* /ˌmi:tiə'rɒlədʒɪst/
meteorology *n* /ˌmi:tiə'rɒlədʒi/
microphone *n* /'maɪkrəˌfəʊn/ *
morning *n* /'mɔ:nɪŋ/ ***
(nobody) else *pron* /ˌ(nəʊbədi) 'els/ ***
North Pole *n* /ˌnɔ:θ 'pəʊl/
on air *phrase* /ˌɒn 'eə/
predict *v* /prɪ'dɪkt/ ***
previous *adj* /'pri:viəs/ ***
programme *n* /'prəʊgræm/ ***
radio producer *n* /'reɪdiəʊ prəˌdju:sə/
rain *n, v* /reɪn/ ***
recognise *v* /'rekəgnaɪz/ ***
schedule *n* /'ʃedju:l/ **
Scotland *n* /'skɒtlənd/
snore *v* /snɔ:/
snow(ing) *v* /'snəʊ(ɪŋ)/
source *n* /sɔ:s/ ***
storm *n* /stɔ:m/ **
stormy *adj* /'stɔ:mi/
story *n* /'stɔ:ri/ ***
studio *n* /'stju:diəʊ/ ***
sunny *adj* /'sʌni/ *
warm *adj* /wɔ:m/ ***
weather *n* /'weðə/ ***
weatherman *n* /'weðəˌmæn/
windy *adj* /'wɪndi/ *
wrong *adj* /rɒŋ/ ***

Unit 4

author *n* /'ɔ:θə/ ***
camera phone *n* /'kæmərə ˌfəʊn/
design *n* /dɪ'zaɪn/ ***
develop *v* /dɪ'veləp/ ***
disappear *v* /ˌdɪsə'pɪə/ ***
electric toothbrush *n* /ɪˌlektrɪk 'tu:θbrʌʃ/
energy *n* /'enədʒi/ ***
fake tan *n* /ˌfeɪk 'tæn/
find out *v* /ˌfaɪnd 'aʊt/
fuel *n* /'fju:əl/ ***
give up *v* /ˌgɪv 'ʌp/
GPS device *n* /ˌdʒi: pi: 'es dɪˌvaɪs/
greenhouse gas *n* /'gri:nhaʊs ˌgæs/
hairdryer *n* /'heəˌdraɪə/
happen *v* /'hæpən/ ***
hard to use *phrase* /ˌhɑ:d tə 'ju:z/
hi-tech *adj* /ˌhaɪ 'tek/
invention *n* /ɪn'venʃn/ **
iPod *n* /'aɪˌpɒd/
kill *v* /kɪl/ ***
listener *n* /'lɪsnə/ *
market *v* /'mɑ:kɪt/ ***
microwave food *n* /'maɪkrəˌweɪv ˌfu:d/
non-alcoholic beer *n* /ˌnɒn ælkəˌhɒlɪk 'bɪə/
normal *adj* /'nɔ:ml/ ***
(not) work out *v* /(ˌnɒt) ˌwɜ:k 'aʊt/
nuclear power *n* /ˌnju:kliə 'paʊə/ *
petrol *n* /'petrəl/ **
remote control *n* /rɪˌməʊt kən'trəʊl/ *
rush into *v* /ˌrʌʃ 'ɪntə/
set up *v* /ˌset 'ʌp/
silly *adj* /'sɪli/ **
sport *n* /spɔ:t/ ***
taste *v* /teɪst/ **
television *n* /'telɪˌvɪʒn/ ***
terrible *adj* /'terəbl/ ***
the Internet *n* /ði 'ɪntəˌnet/ ***
toothbrush *n* /'tu:θˌbrʌʃ/
try sth out *v* /ˌtraɪ ... 'aʊt/
vote *v* /vəʊt/ ***
water *n* /'wɔ:tə/ ***

Communication activities

Student A

Unit 1, Speaking Ex 1 page 69

1 Look at the pictures. You are a tourist. What do you want to know in each situation? Act out the conversations with your partner. Start each conversation with 'Excuse me, ...?'

2 Read the rolecards. Your partner will start the conversations. Listen and give your partner the information he / she asks for.

Rolecard 1

You are a ticket inspector at Newcastle station in New South Wales, Australia. You are waiting for the next train to Sydney to arrive at the platform. The train leaves Newcastle at 18.30 and the journey takes 3 hours.

Rolecard 2

You are at a bus stop in Paris. You are waiting for the next bus to the Louvre museum. You do not know what time the next bus is, but you know that there is a bus every 20 minutes. It's number 212. You can buy a ticket from the driver.

Unit 2, Speaking and vocabulary Ex 2 page 70

CHOICES Listening scripts

Unit 1 See the world

Listening script 01

Reading text from page 67

Listening script 02

Language study Ex 6 from page 68

Listening script 03

1

A: Next, please.
B: A ticket to Oxford, please.
A: Single or return?
B: Return, please.
A: That's £15.99. The next train leaves from platform two in 20 minutes.
B: Thank you.

2

C: Excuse me, is this the right stop for Blackheath?
D: Yes, it is. You can take the number 54 or the number 89.
C: Thank you. When's the next bus?
D: In about 10 minutes, I think.

3

E: Excuse me, which gate does the flight to Warsaw leave from?
F: Gate 26. That's in terminal 2.
E: Thank you.

4

G: Excuse me, is this the right platform for the train to Bristol?
H: Yes, it is.
G: Thank you. And when does the train arrive in Bristol?
H: At half past six.

5

I: Victoria, please.
J: Here you are.
I: Thank you. How long does the bus take to get there?
J: About half an hour. But it depends on the traffic.

6

K: Can I see your passport, please?
L: Here you are.
K: Here's your boarding pass. Your seat's in row 20, next to the window.
L: Is the plane on time?
K: Yes, it is. You can board at gate 14 in twenty minutes.

Listening script 04

1 A ticket to Oxford, please.
2 Excuse me, is this the right stop for Blackheath?
3 When's the next bus?
4 Which gate does the flight to Warsaw leave from?
5 Is this the right platform for the train to Bristol?
6 When does the train arrive in Bristol?
7 How long does the bus take to get there?
8 Is the plane on time?

Unit 2 Market place

Listening script 05

(T= Tanya, S = sales assistant)

S: Good afternoon. Can I help you?
T: Yes, please. I want to buy a digital camera.
S: Have you got any particular camera in mind?
T: No, not really. What would you recommend?
S: Well, that depends. How much do you want to spend?
T: Not more than about £150.
S: OK. And what do you want it for?
T: Well, to take on holiday, to take photos at parties – that kind of thing.
S: Right. This Snapshot is a nice little model. It comes with a 512MB memory card. For a good quality camera it really isn't expensive at £149.99.
T: I see. What about that one over there? The one that costs £99.
S: Ah yes. The Quickflick. It's a good camera too and it's on offer at £99. It's a bit bigger and heavier than the Snapshot, but it takes better quality pictures.
T: Is it difficult to use?
S: Well, it's a bit more difficult to use than the Snapshot. The Snapshot is fully automatic and it's very easy to use.
T: Can I have a look at them?
S: Yes, of course. Look ... the Quickflick has got a larger screen than the Snapshot. It's got a smaller memory card though. Only 64MB. You can buy more memory, of course, but it's rather expensive.
T: I see. Well, I think I'll go on looking. Thank you very much, anyway.
S: You're welcome. Have a nice day.

Listening script 06

Reading text from page 73

Unit 3 Outdoor life

Listening script 07

Rain before seven, fine before eleven.
Evening red and morning grey, are sure signs of a fine day.
Evening grey and morning red, put on your hat or you'll wet your head.
Red sky at night, shepherds' delight.
When spiders weave their webs by noon, fine weather is coming soon.
Flies will swarm before a storm.

Listening script 08

Reading text from page 75

Listening script 09

1

Good afternoon from the Maracana Stadium in Rio. It's a cold day here today for this friendly match between two great football teams – Japan and Brazil. There's a strong wind blowing in from the north and it's raining hard. We're waiting for the teams to come out onto the pitch and start playing.

2

This is Christine Wakefield here in Sydney, for the Davis Cup semi-finals. It's a good day for tennis today. It's warm but cloudy and a light breeze is blowing. That's good news for tennis fans. Over to court one where the young mixed doubles pair from Belarus are just going into the second set.

3

I'm sorry to say that it's a bad day here for the skiers at the Winter Olympics. It's snowing and the slopes are covered in fog. Unless things clear within the next hour, it looks as if today's races will be called off.

4

Good morning from this year's Grand Prix in Budapest. Although the race doesn't start until 12, crowds are already arriving in the boiling sun. It's extremely hot here, with temperatures up in the high 90s.

Unit 4 Advances

Listening script 10

(P = presenter, R = reporter, T – Tony,
A = Annette)

P: This month on *Advances* we're celebrating the wonderful world of inventions in a series of programmes. Our reporter, Nicky Moody, has been asking a number of British inventors about their favourite and least favourite new inventions. This week she spoke to Tony Brians and Annette Wilson. Tony works in the research and development department of a well-known music publishing company, and Annette is an inventor for an international electronics firm.

R: Thank you for finding the time to talk to us today, Tony. What's your favourite new invention?

T: Without a doubt, for me it's my iPod. I love it! I have a huge collection of records and CDs - and I don't know where to put them. Now all my music is on my iPod and I can take it everywhere with me. I travel a lot in my job, so that's great. The only problem is that last year – by mistake – I wiped all the music off the memory. It took me three months to put it all on again. I've got 26 days of listening on this iPod, you know.

R: Thank you, Tony. Now, Annette, could you tell me about your least favourite modern invention?

A: My least favourite invention. Of course – that's easy. It's the remote control for the TV – for all sorts of reasons. My husband loves watching sports, you see. I don't. And when I want to change the channel, I can never find the remote control because my husband always hides it! Also, he sometimes watches TV all day and he doesn't get up even once to change the channel in all that time. It's a terrible invention!

P: Now, before we hear more from Annette and Tony, remember we're also interested in our listeners' ideas. To tell us your opinion, go to our website at the usual address, that's worldradio/advances.uk and click on inventions.

Listening script 11

1 hairdryer, where, email, compare
2 device, favourite, high tech, iPod
3 phone, remote, world, control
4 email, same, fake, camera
5 microwave, power, hour, about
6 choices, noisy, television, boy
7 year, nuclear, beer, idea

Listening script 12

Reading text from page 80

Unit 5 Review

Listening script 13

I grew up in London, a very long time ago.
I remember my father's first car. It was light brown and it had a seat at the back – right at the back on the outside. I loved riding in that seat. It was windy and not very comfortable, but I saw everything as we drove along. It's a pity modern cars don't have seats like that any more – but cars go much faster nowadays, I suppose.
I was only a boy when World War II started. It was very dangerous to stay in the city, so they sent all the children to live in the countryside. My school went all the way to Cornwall, in the south-west of England. It was a long, long way and I didn't see my parents for three years.
I remember the journey. It was my first time on a train. My mother took me to the railway station. The whole train was full of children going to the country. In my carriage we were all boys - there were 10 of us on a seat for three people. The journey was very long and uncomfortable. Trains were very slow in those days, you know.
The school was very beautiful, but the weather in Cornwall was horrible. It was often very cold and windy, I remember. And I saw snow for the first time when I was there, too. We usually had a lot of snow in December and January down in Cornwall. It was better than London in some ways though, because it wasn't foggy there – just cold. In London it was always raining or foggy – and very bad for you.
Another thing that I remember well is the first time I saw a television. I think I was nine or ten. Televisions then were very expensive, and the screens were small and difficult to see. It was unusual for people to have them at home – but a friend of my parents had one. The picture was black and white, of course.
Sometimes I think about all the changes that I've seen in my life, and I just can't believe it.

Listening script 14

Song from page 84

Communication activities

Student B

Unit 1, Speaking Ex 1 page 69

1 Read the rolecards. Your partner will start the conversations. Listen and give your partner the information he / she asks for.

2 Look at the pictures. You are a tourist. What do you want to know in each situation? Act out the conversations with your partner. Start each conversation with *'Excuse me, ...'*.

Rolecard 1

You are waiting at a bus stop for the next bus to Green Park in London. The buses usually run every 15 minutes. The journey takes about half an hour, depending on the traffic. A single ticket costs £2.

Rolecard 2

You work for Thai Airways in Japan. You are at the check-in desk at the airport checking passengers in for the next Thai Airways flight to Bangkok. It leaves from gate 15 at 14.55. At the moment the flight is on time. It takes 7 hours to fly to Bangkok.

Unit 2, Speaking Ex 1 page 73

1 Your teacher will give you a number. Read about your new product

1. Sleeping drink: this fizzy drink tastes like lemonade and helps you sleep at night – or any time during the day when you need a rest.
2. Magazine on a water bottle: take off the label from this new brand of bottled water and you find a 32-page magazine under it. It's about fashion, health and beauty.
3. Pass your exam pills: these pills contain vitamins and minerals which are good for your memory. Take one pill a day and pass all your exams.
4. Exercise in your sleep: for people with no time to go to the gym. You wear this exercise suit instead of pyjamas. As you sleep, the suit exercises your muscles.

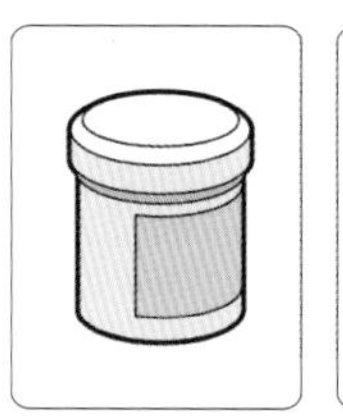

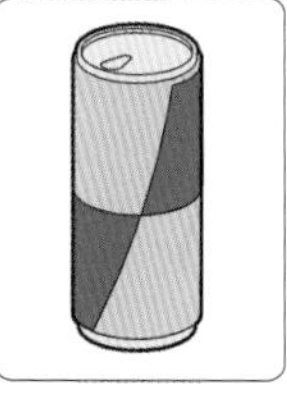

2 Complete the notes about your product and decide why your company should make it.

Example:

GROW HAIR BODY CREAM

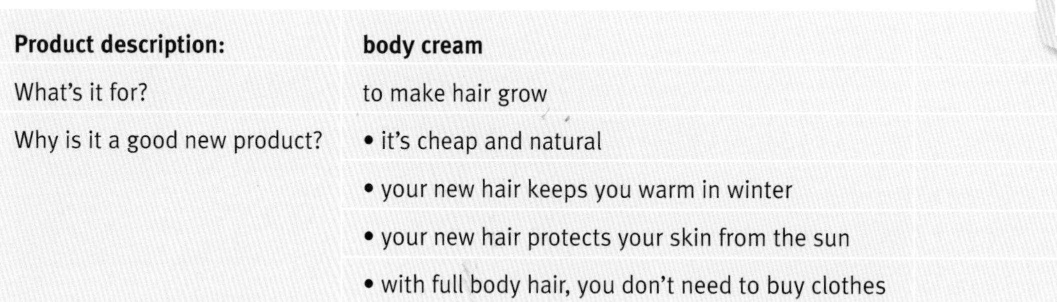

Product description:	**body cream**
What's it for?	to make hair grow
Why is it a good new product?	• it's cheap and natural
	• your new hair keeps you warm in winter
	• your new hair protects your skin from the sun
	• with full body hair, you don't need to buy clothes

3 Present your product to your group. Decide on the best new product. Each group can only chose <u>one</u> new product.